A MARRIAGE WITHOUT REGRETS

PRECEPTS FOR LIFE

with Kay Arthur

™

"AND SO THEY LIVED HAPPILY EVER AFTER!"

What happened to yesterday's fairy tale ending? Today we're living every other "ending," a time when marriage is devalued, minimized, trivialized, even scorned. The commitment to stay married in spite of poverty, sickness, and "worse" things has been replaced with "so long as it works well for me!" Fuses are short, anger long and bitter. Separation and divorce are rampant. Alternatives like "living together" last only a short time. Warring genders seek out their own sex for comfort (homosexuality). Children are major liabilities many prefer to do without.

Why has our culture abandoned marriage? There's a simple answer to this. Our society has rejected marriage because it has rejected the God of truth who created not only the covenant of marriage but also the very genders to enter into the contract. Today these truths and principles of God's eternal Word are rejected, mocked, belittled, or just plain ignored. And we've inherited all the heartache, isolation, regret, guilt, loneliness and hopelessness that accompany the rejection of a personal God. We're alienated first from God and then from each other.

It doesn't have to be this way in your life, beloved. The eternal Word we turned away from is the way out—the path to not just a marriage but also a life without regrets. Jesus said "I am the way, and the truth, and the life; no one comes to the Father but through me" (John 14:6).

I took this "way" a long time ago and have never looked back. Following it entails courage to swim upstream, go against the grain, reject status quo. It means taking a stand against a culture that has taken particular aim at God's first two covenants—life and marriage. It means defying majority belief, standing up for absolutes in a relativistic culture.

God promises more than just "no regrets." Jesus said He came so that his sheep "may have life and have it abundantly" (John 10:10). That means abundant marriages too, abundant relationships generally, a new family, a new future, a new you.

If you're married or are planning to marry, I know you want a marriage without regrets, an abundant marriage filled with love, trust, hope and great memories. I have a lot to share with you because I failed miserably the first time around when I was an unbeliever. Jesus changed all that; He raised me out of the living death I was "living." Join me in this study of His Word. Let's renew our hope together!

Kay

1	Program Lessons
114	Discover Truth
118	How Do I Start Studying the Bible?
120	About Precept

Visit precept.org/resource for more Free Bible Study Resources!

PRECEPTS FOR LIFE™
Study Companion

This Bible study material was designed for use with the TV and Radio teaching program, Precepts for Life™ with renowned Bible study teacher Kay Arthur, a production of Precept Ministries International. This inductive 30-minute daily Bible study program airs on many satellite, cable, and broadcast stations, and on the internet at **www.preceptsforlife.com.**

As with all Inductive Bible studies, the best way to use the material is to complete the assignments in each lesson before listening or watching the PFL program for that day. These programs are also available on DVD and CD at **www.preceptsforlife.com** or by phone (1.800.763.1990 for television viewers or 1.800.734.7707 for radio listeners). For more information about the Precept Inductive Bible Study Method and Precept Ministries International, visit **www.preceptsforlife.com.**

These materials are also useful for Bible study apart from the Precepts for Life™ programs. We hope you'll find them valuable for studying God's Word and that your walk will be strengthened by the life-changing Truth you'll encounter each day.

A Marriage Without Regrets STUDY COMPANION
Published by Precept Ministries of Reach Out, Inc.
P. O. Box 182218
Chattanooga, TN 37422

ISBN–13: 978-1-62119-413-2

Scripture quotations are from the New American Standard Bible, ©1960, 1962, 1963, 1968, 1971, 1972, 1973, 1975, 1977, 1995 by the Lockman Foundation. Used by permission. www.lockman.org

Introduction

PROGRAM 1

TODAY'S TEXTS

Genesis 1:26-28

Revelation 4:11

1 Corinthians 8:5-6

Genesis 2:7; 2:18-21

Galatians 3:28

1 Corinthians 11:7-12; 11:3

INTRODUCTION

When I was eighteen years old, I used to stand in the dorm room of St. Luke's School of Nursing in Cleveland, Ohio, and look out over the city. And I would think, what's going on in that home? What's happening between that man and that woman? What's happening with those children? And then I would think about the day that I would be married. I had wonderful dreams of marriage. I had the scenario and then I got married and that marriage ended in divorce. Precious one, don't you want a marriage without regrets? And the first principle I want to share with you today in this series on marriage is the fact that if you are going to have a marriage without regrets, it begins with you. It begins with understanding who you are.

DID YOU KNOW?

Genesis 2:18: "I will make him a helper suitable [נֶגֶד *neged*] for him."

1 Corinthians 11:12: You'll notice that the NASB's *has his birth* is in italics. Literally the verse reads: "For as the woman out of [ἐκ: **ek**] the man so also the man *through* [διὰ: *dia*] the woman."

QUESTIONS

1. Read Genesis 1:26-28 marking **man** and all pronouns with a black stick figure.

    a. What in the text tells us that "man" is not Adam only? (Carefully check the use of all pronouns.)

    b. From this fact, what can we say about male and female? Are they equal or unequal? Are they both made in God's image?

    c. What are they both to do according to verse 28?

    d. Why does the text say "<u>our</u> image" in v. 26 and "<u>His</u> own image" in v. 27? What do these tell us about God's nature?

2. Now read Revelation 4:11.

    a. Are we "accidents"? Did we "just happen" for no reason at all? Do we have a destiny? Who or what guarantees this?

    b. Did God *want* to create you? What do you think He wants *from* you?

    c. What does this say (one way or the other) about your value? Who values you *first* and *most*?

3. Now carefully observe 1 Corinthians 8:6.

   a. How do we relate to the one God and the one Lord? What has each done for us?

4. Now read Genesis 2:7, 18, and 19-21.

   a. What did God make the male out of according to v. 7?

   b. Why did God make a female according to v. 18? What does "suitable" mean? (See **Did You Know?**)

   c. What did God fashion the woman out of? Is this part of the body *significant* as compared to others He could have used?

5. Read Galatians 3:28. What does "neither male nor female; for you are all one in Christ Jesus" mean? In what sense are the male and female "one"?

6. Now read 1 Corinthians 11:7-12.

   a. What are the man and the woman respectively the glory of?

   b. Does man originate from the woman (v. 8)? How can you reconcile this verse with verse 12's "so also the man *has his birth* through the woman"? (See **Did You Know?**)

7. Finally, read 1 Corinthians 11:3.

   a. Who is the head of every man?

   b. Who is the head of the woman?

   c. Who is the head of Christ?

Prayer

Father, Your creation is so glorious and Your designs so perfect. Your Word is so clear that this perfection is Your plan from eternity. I praise You for creating mankind male and female, equal in Your sight. I praise You for making us both in Your holy and righteous image. I praise You for Your will, Your immutable counsel that gives us our very being and purpose. Lord, help me to keep these truths always in mind. Help me to be the perfect man or perfect woman by delighting in Your will and walking in Your ways, to the glory of Your Son the Lord Jesus. In His name I pray, Amen.

Today's Texts

Genesis 1:26-28

26 Then God said, "Let Us make man in Our image, according to Our likeness; and let them rule over the fish of the sea and over the birds of the sky and over the cattle and over all the earth, and over every creeping thing that creeps on the earth."

27 God created man in His own image, in the image of God He created him; male and female He created them.

28 God blessed them; and God said to them, Be fruitful and multiply, and fill the earth, and subdue it; and rule over the fish of the sea and over the birds of the sky and over every living thing that moves on the earth."

1 Corinthians 8:6

6 yet for us there is *but* one God, the Father, from whom are all things and we *exist* for Him; and one Lord, Jesus Christ, by whom are all things, and we *exist* through Him.

Genesis 2:7, 18-21

7 Then the LORD God formed man of dust from the ground, and breathed into his nostrils the breath of life; and man became a living being.

18 Then the LORD God said, "It is not good for the man to be alone; I will make him a helper suitable for him."

19 Out of the ground the LORD God formed every beast of the field and every bird of the sky, and brought them to the man to see what he would call them; and whatever the man called a living creature, that was its name.

20 The man gave names to all the cattle, and to the birds of the sky, and to every beast of the field, but for Adam there was not found a helper suitable for him.

21 So the LORD God caused a deep sleep to fall upon the man, and he slept; then He took one of his ribs and closed up the flesh at that place.

Galatians 3:28

28 There is neither Jew nor Greek, there is neither slave nor free man, there is neither male nor female; for you are all one in Christ Jesus.

1 Corinthians 11:7-12

7 For a man ought not to have his head covered, since he is the image and glory of God; but the woman is the glory of man.

8 For man does not originate from woman, but woman from man;

9 for indeed man was not created for the woman's sake, but woman for the man's sake.

10 Therefore the woman ought to have *a symbol of* authority on her head, because of the angels.

11 However, in the Lord, neither is woman independent of man, nor is man independent of woman.

12 For as the woman originates from the man, so also the man has his birth through the woman; and all things originate from God.

1 Corinthians 11:3

3 But I want you to understand that Christ is the head of every man, and the man is the head of a woman, and God is the head of Christ.

PROGRAM 2

Differences of Men and Women

INTRODUCTION

He created them equal. 1 Peter chapter 3 tells a man that he is to "live with his wife in an understanding way since both of them are joint heirs of God." In other words, God is not partial to one sex over the other sex, although He made them different.

QUESTIONS

1. Read Genesis 2:23.

   a. Why was Eve called "woman?" (See **Did You Know?**)

   b. What does "out of" imply in terms of rank and/or equality?

2. Now read 1 Peter 3:7 (See the NASB's marginal note for "someone weaker" and then **Did You Know?**)

   a. In what ways are women "weaker vessels"?

   b. Does the conjoined phrase "*live with* [them] in an *understanding* way" bear on the meaning? Does Paul have something more than *physical* in mind?

   c. Among other reasons, why are men to honor their wives according to this verse? What are they in God's eyes? Is this a *temporal* or *eternal* honor? Which of the two has the higher rank?

TODAY'S TEXTS

Genesis 2:23
1 Peter 3:7

DID YOU KNOW?

Genesis 2:23: "She shall be called *woman* אִשָּׁה (*isha*) because from man מֵאִישׁ (*meish*) she was taken."

The Old English *wifmann* (female man) slowly evolved to our modern-day "woman."

1 Peter 3:7: "someone weaker," literally weaker [ἀσθενεστέρῳ] vessel [σκεύει].

While the term *vessel* is ordinarily a physical container like a jar (Luke 8:16) or a body (1 Thessalonians 4:4), the sources of bodily weakness are not always *physical* factors like the size of a muscle or sickness.

The Greek term for "weak" (*asthenia*) frequently substitutes for spiritual factors like *fear* (Heb. 11:34), *guilt* (Rom. 14:2), and *doubt* (Rom. 4:19; 14:1; see also Heb. 4:5; 7:18; 7:28)—all which impact the body negatively.

As always, here we have to determine the meanings of terms from their contexts.

Prayer

Father, thank you for creating men and women. We praise you for the different strengths that complement one another in this life and for the honor of equal inheritance of the grace of life that will extend into eternity. Help us to live with each other in understanding ways, sympathizing and complementing so that our prayers will be effective. In Jesus' name, Amen!

Today's Texts

Genesis 2:23

23 The man said, "This is now bone of my bones, and flesh of my flesh; she shall be called woman, because she was taken out of man."

1 Peter 3:7

7 You husbands in the same way, live with *your wives* in an understanding way, as with someone weaker, since she is a woman; and show her honor as a fellow heir of the grace of life, so that your prayers will not be hindered.

PROGRAM **3**

Purpose of Marriage

TODAY'S TEXTS

Genesis 1:28

Hebrews 13:4

Ephesians 5:25-32

Deuteronomy 22:28-29

INTRODUCTION

If God knows that there's going to be divorce, wouldn't it be better for us to not marry but just live together? Wouldn't it be better to do what we're doing and that is to move in with one another to try each other out for a while and see if this is really going to work, see if we really want to make this commitment? Well, that's the thinking of the world. But it is not according to the Word of God.

QUESTIONS

1. Read Genesis 1:28. What are God's purposes for marriage according to the text? List the verbs.

2. Now read Hebrews 13:4.
   a. How does a couple keep their marriage bed "undefiled"?

   b. According to the text, why don't options to marriage work?

3. Read Ephesians 5:25-32.
   a. How are husbands supposed to love their wives?

   b. What did Jesus do for His Church that a husband should do for his wife?

   c. What is "this mystery" (v. 32) according to the context? What does marriage model that is so important to do?

4. Finally, read Deuteronomy 22:28-29. If a man seizes a virgin who is not engaged and lies with her,
   a. What does he *have* to do?

   b. What can he *never* do?

Prayer

Father, thank you for the beautiful picture of Christ's love for His Bride, the Church, that you've created in marriage. Thank you for putting me into Your family by making me part of Jesus' Bride through faith. Help me keep this bed undefiled by turning from the adultery of idolatry. Lord, I know there are no sexual options to marriage according to Your Word, so guard me from fornicating and adulterating with other people as well. I want to be pure in spirit and in body. Confirm me to the end blameless in the Day of the Lord Jesus. Amen!

Today's Texts

Genesis 1:28

28 God blessed them; and God said to them, "Be fruitful and multiply, and fill the earth, and subdue it; and rule over the fish of the sea and over the birds of the sky and over every living thing that moves on the earth."

Hebrews 13:4

4 Marriage is to be held in honor among all, and the marriage bed is to be undefiled; for fornicators and adulterers God will judge.

Ephesians 5:25-32

25 Husbands, love your wives, just as Christ also loved the church and gave Himself up for her,

26 so that He might sanctify her, having cleansed her by the washing of water with the word,

27 that He might present to Himself the church in all her glory, having no spot or wrinkle or any such thing; but that she would be holy and blameless.

28 So husbands ought also to love their own wives as their own bodies. He who loves his own wife loves himself;

29 for no one ever hated his own flesh, but nourishes and cherishes it, just as Christ also does the church,

30 because we are members of His body.

31 FOR THIS REASON A MAN SHALL LEAVE HIS FATHER AND MOTHER AND SHALL BE JOINED TO HIS WIFE, AND THE TWO SHALL BECOME ONE FLESH.

32 This mystery is great; but I am speaking with reference to Christ and the church.

Deuteronomy 22:28-29

28 "If a man finds a girl who is a virgin, who is not engaged, and seizes her and lies with her and they are discovered,

29 then the man who lay with her shall give to the girl's father fifty shekels of silver, and she shall become his wife because he has violated her; he cannot divorce her all his days.

PROGRAM **4**

TODAY'S TEXTS

Mark 8:31-34

Luke 14:26

Ephesians 4:31—5:2

The Master Key

INTRODUCTION

Precious One, this is the master key, the master key to life. The master key to a marriage without regrets is for you Precious One to so fall in love with God, to so get to know this Word which is pure unadulterated truth.

QUESTIONS

1. Read Mark 8:31-34.
   a. What was Peter trying to do? Can we save our loved ones?

   b. How did Jesus respond to Peter's attempt?

   c. Does Satan have God's or man's interests in mind? Do you think he's interested in man's *good*?

   d. What must we do to follow Christ? Is it an easy path? What's more "natural" for us to do, deny or affirm ourselves?

2. Now read Luke 14:26.
   a. How is a person to hate "his own life"? How can we reconcile this with Jesus' command to love our neighbors as our*selves*?

   b. Who should be our first love?

3. Finally, read Ephesians 4:31—5:2.

   a. Does 4:31 help us understand hating our own "soul" (the old man)?

   b. According to 5:1 what should characterize the new man, the new creature in Christ? Is this new man the one we should love, as the basis for loving others?

c. Who are we called to "imitate"?

d. According to 5:2, how did Jesus express His love? Did He deny Himself? How? Is this part of what we should "imitate"?

Prayer

Father, You've called me to love my neighbor as myself and yet hate my own self. I realize that while I'm a new creature in Christ I still have the old man living in my flesh. Lord, I need your Spirit and Word to overpower and put to death this flesh and bring me more into conformity with Jesus, who denied Himself fully and took up a cross to save all men. I know that self-sacrifice is not easy because it's not natural, in fact as Your Word says "With men this [salvation] is impossible" (Matthew 19:26) But the same Word says "But with God all things are possible" and so I look to You to save me from sin and make me more like Your son every day until the day I'm called into His presence. In His name I pray, Amen!

Today's Texts

Mark 8:31-34

31 And He began to teach them that the Son of Man must suffer many things and be rejected by the elders and the chief priests and the scribes, and be killed, and after three days rise again.

32 And He was stating the matter plainly. And Peter took Him aside and began to rebuke Him.

33 But turning around and seeing His disciples, He rebuked Peter and said, "Get behind Me, Satan; for you are not setting your mind on God's interests, but man's."

34 And He summoned the crowd with His disciples, and said to them, "If anyone wishes to come after Me, he must deny himself, and take up his cross and follow Me.

Luke 14:26

26 "If anyone comes to Me, and does not hate his own father and mother and wife and children and brothers and sisters, yes, and even his own life, he cannot be My disciple.

Ephesians 4:31—5:2

31 Let all bitterness and wrath and anger and clamor and slander be put away from you, along with all malice.

32 Be kind to one another, tender-hearted, forgiving each other, just as God in Christ also has forgiven you.

1 Therefore be imitators of God, as beloved children;

2 and walk in love, just as Christ also loved you and gave Himself up for us, an offering and a sacrifice to God as a fragrant aroma.

PROGRAM 5

Lies That Women Believe

TODAY'S TEXTS

2 Timothy 3:16

2 Peter 1:20-21

Psalm 12:6

1 Timothy 5:14

Titus 2:3-5

DID YOU KNOW?

1 Timothy 5:14: "keep house" οἰκοδεσποτεῖν (from *oikos* [house] and *despoteo* [rule; we get our English "despot" from this term]).

Titus 2:5 "workers at home" (οἰςκουργοὺς from *oikos* [house] and *ourgos* [worker]).

INTRODUCTION

What have I done wrong? Why am I so messed up? Why am I so frustrated? Why am I torn in all these different pieces? He wants to show us where we're wrong. But He doesn't leave you there, Precious One. It's also profitable for correction. He shows us how to take what's wrong and make it right. He doesn't just throw us away because we've messed up. He doesn't just say, "That's it kid, you've had it, you've blown it." No. He says, 'Come here. I'm your father."

QUESTIONS

1. Read 2 Timothy 3:16, 2 Peter 1:21, and Psalm 12:6. Mark all the characteristics of the **Word of God** with a purple open book shaded green and then list them here.

2. From all the above . . .
   a. Does God's Word contain lies or factual errors?

   b. Is it man's opinion?

   c. Now read 1 Timothy 5:14 red underlining what Paul commends the **younger women** to do. List these things here:

   d. Finally, read Titus 2:3-5 red underlining what Paul commends the **older women** to do and red shading the two **"so that"s.** List his commendations here:

   e. What is the first purpose of these commands?

Prayer

Father, I rejoice in Your Word that lightens darkness and injects truth into our culture of lies. Thank you for breathing Your pure Word without dross, without error, into holy men who wrote it down so I could be taught, reproved, corrected, trained, and equipped for every good work. Lord, help me encourage young women to pray for husbands and—as Paul birthed children through the Gospel (1 Corinthians 4:15)—to raise up spiritual seed for Your kingdom whether they marry or not. Help me encourage older married women to love their husbands and children so Your Word will not be dishonored. Help me encourage widows to live out the high calling of Anna who at 84 years old never left the temple, serving night and day with fastings and prayers (Luke 2:37). Help us all to be reverent, sensible, and pure. In Jesus' name, Amen!

Today's Texts

2 Timothy 3:16-17

16 All Scripture is inspired by God and profitable for teaching, for reproof, for correction, for training in righteousness;

17 so that the man of God may be adequate, equipped for every good work.

2 Peter 1:20-21

20 But know this first of all, that no prophecy of Scripture is *a matter* of one's own interpretation,

21 for no prophecy was ever made by an act of human will, but men moved by the Holy Spirit spoke from God.

Psalm 12:6

6 The words of the LORD are pure words; As silver tried in a furnace on the earth, refined seven times.

1 Timothy 5:14

14 Therefore, I want younger *widows* to get married, bear children, keep house, *and* give the enemy no occasion for reproach;

Titus 2:3-5

3 Older women likewise are to be reverent in their behavior, not malicious gossips nor enslaved to much wine, teaching what is good,

4 so that they may encourage the young women to love their husbands, to love their children,

5 *to be* sensible, pure, workers at home, kind, being subject to their own husbands, so that the word of God will not be dishonored.

PROGRAM **6**

TODAY'S TEXTS
Proverbs 6:26-32; 7:25-27

CROSS-REFERENCES
Leviticus 20:10

More Lies That Women Believe

INTRODUCTION

Precious One, know this: that with God there's a new beginning. With God there is hope. With God there is no failure. The failure has becomes a thing of the past—no failures, only a future. The Word of God says in the Old Testament (and I know that Jesus is saying it to you today): "I know the plans I have for you, plans for good and not for evil. To give you a future and to give you hope."

QUESTIONS

1. Read Proverbs 6:26-32 mark **harlot** with a red "H" and **adulteress** and its respective synonyms, pronouns, and associated terms which refer to her with a red "A".

   a. What's the huntress's preference, a wealthy or poor man? What does harlotry lead a man to?

   b. What two images does Solomon use to show that harlotry has bad results that are inevitable?

   c. How does the punishment for the adulterer contrast with that for the thief according to the text? (See **Cross-reference** Leviticus 20:10.)

2. Now read Proverbs 7:25-27 marking the female pronouns that refer to the adulteress (from v. 5) with a red "A".

   a. What do you think the "ways" and "paths" of an adulteress are?

   b. Why is the adulteress's way/path dangerous? What happens to her "victims"?

Prayer

Father, guard my thoughts, my eyes, and my actions from seeking fornication and adultery. Give me advance warning if I stray even close to one of these paths that lead to death. Stop me from thinking thoughts that frustrate me and also hurt my neighbor if I carry them out to actions. Give me a single mind that values and a holy heart that desires your beauty more than anything on this earth (Psalm 27:4). If I'm going to lust as the deer pants for the water brooks, then let its object be only You (Psalm 42:1). In Jesus' mighty Name, Amen!

Today's Texts

Proverbs 6:26-32

26 For on account of a harlot one is reduced to a loaf of bread, and an adulteress hunts for the precious life.

27 Can a man take fire in his bosom and his clothes not be burned?

28 Or can a man walk on hot coals and his feet not be scorched?

29 So is the one who goes in to his neighbor's wife; whoever touches her will not go unpunished.

30 Men do not despise a thief if he steals to satisfy himself when he is hungry;

31 But when he is found, he must repay sevenfold; he must give all the substance of his house.

32 The one who commits adultery with a woman is lacking sense; he who would destroy himself does it.

Proverbs 7:25-27

25 Do not let your heart turn aside to her ways, do not stray into her paths.

26 For many are the victims she has cast down, and numerous are all her slain.

27 Her house is the way to Sheol, descending to the chambers of death.

Leviticus 20:10

10 If *there* is a man who commits adultery with another man's wife, one who commits adultery with his friend's wife, the adulterer and adulteress shall be put to death.

PROGRAM 7

TODAY'S TEXTS
Genesis 2:22-25
Ephesians 5:22-33
1 Corinthians 11:3; 7-9
Matthew 19:3-12
Romans 7:2-3

CROSS-REFERENCES
1 Corinthians 6:16

DID YOU KNOW?
Glory δόξα from the verb *dokeo*: to value, think, suppose, assume.

Essential Factors for a Marital Foundation

INTRODUCTION

Listen, no matter how angry you get, no matter how frustrated you become, Beloved, don't say the "D" word. Don't talk about divorce. Don't talk about separation. Don't let it be in your vocabulary. Why? Because marriage is permanent. Jesus says this in Matthew chapter 19.

QUESTIONS

1. **Stewardship.** Read Genesis 2:22-25 marking *man* and respective pronouns with a stick figures.

   a. Did God give Eve to Adam? What verb implies this?

   b. What are we to do with things God gives us? What kind of accountability do we have for them?

   c. What accountabilities to the woman does the man have?

2. **Identification.** Now read Ephesians 5:22-33 marking *love(s)(d)* and associated terms with a red shaded heart.

   a. How is a man to love his own wife?

   b. How do men generally treat their bodies according to the text?

   c. What analogies are there <u>between</u> a man and his wife <u>and</u> Christ and His Church? What *is* the Church and what does Jesus *do* for it?

3. **Headship.** Read 1 Corinthians 11:3 and then 7-9 red underlining all terms related to <u>rank</u>.

   a. How do the three headships in v. 3 help us explain what "head" means?

   b. What is man "the image and glory" of?

c. What is the woman "the glory" of?

d. What is "glory" (See **Did You Know?**) How is the woman the "value" of the man?

4. **Permanence.** Read Matthew 19:3-12 marking *divorce* plus synonyms and pronouns with two overlapping side-by-side circles with a black line through them. Then read Romans 7:2-3.

   a. What does Jesus say about divorce? What does the Law "say" compared to what Moses "permitted."

   b. Why did Moses "permit" the issuance of a certificate of divorce? Is "Moses permitted" the same as "God commanded"? What contrast does Jesus immediately bring up?

   c. Did Jesus allow for any exceptions? If so, what?

   d. How long is marriage for according to Paul in Romans?

5. **Unity.** Now re-read Genesis 2:24, Matthew 19:5-6 and **Cross-reference** 1 Corinthians 6:16 marking *one flesh* and *one body* with a red number 1.

   a. What unity is God seeking in a marriage?

   b. How does 1 Corinthians 6:16 help us expand or limit the meaning of "one"?

6. **Transparency.** Re-read Genesis 2:25.

   a. What do the terms in the phrase *naked and not ashamed* imply with respect to the man, the woman, and God?

   b. According to 3:10, what did the man hide himself from and why?

Prayer

Father, thank You for these five precious truths about marriage. I know that since they apply to Your Son's Bride, His Church, that they apply to me whether I'm married or not. Either way, Lord, help me to steward all the gifts You have given me to serve this Bride, to identify with Jesus' love for His Church, to submit to His headship, to rest secure in the permanence of His love knowing that love never fails, to seek unity with all those who are "one spirit" in the Lord because they are joined to Him (1 Corinthians 6:17), and to be transparent to You, knowing that all things are naked and opened to Your eyes. Thank You for including me in Your Bride so that I'm never alone or forsaken. In Jesus' name, Amen.

Today's Texts

Genesis 2:22-25

22 The LORD God fashioned into a woman the rib which He had taken from the man, and brought her to the man.

23 The man said, "This is now bone of my bones, and flesh of my flesh; she shall be called Woman, because she was taken out of man."

24 For this reason a man shall leave his father and his mother, and be joined to his wife; and they shall become one flesh.

25 And the man and his wife were both naked and were not ashamed.

Ephesians 5:22-33

22 Wives, be subject to your own husbands, as to the Lord.

23 For the husband is the head of the wife, as Christ also is the head of the church, He Himself being the Savior of the body.

24 But as the church is subject to Christ, so also the wives ought to be to their husbands in everything.

25 Husbands, love your wives, just as Christ also loved the church and gave Himself up for her,

26 so that He might sanctify her, having cleansed her by the washing of water with the word,

27 that He might present to Himself the church in all her glory, having no spot or wrinkle or any such thing; but that she would be holy and blameless.

28 So husbands ought also to love their own wives as their own bodies. He who loves his own wife loves himself;

29 for no one ever hated his own flesh, but nourishes and cherishes it, just as Christ also does the church,

30 because we are members of His body.

31 FOR THIS REASON A MAN SHALL LEAVE HIS FATHER AND MOTHER AND SHALL BE JOINED TO HIS WIFE, AND THE TWO SHALL BECOME ONE FLESH.

32 This mystery is great; but I am speaking with reference to Christ and the church.

33 Nevertheless, each individual among you also is to love his own wife even as himself, and the wife must see to it that she respects her husband.

1 Corinthians 11:3, 7-9

3 But I want you to understand that Christ is the head of every man, and the man is the head of a woman, and God is the head of Christ.

7 For a man ought not to have his head covered, since he is the image and glory of God; but the woman is the glory of man.

8 For man does not originate from woman, but woman from man;

9 for indeed man was not created for the woman's sake, but woman for the man's sake.

Matthew 19:3-12

3 Some Pharisees came to Jesus, testing Him and asking, "Is it lawful for a man to divorce his wife for any reason at all?"

4 And He answered and said, "Have you not read that He who created them from the beginning MADE THEM MALE AND FEMALE,

5 and said, 'FOR THIS REASON A MAN SHALL LEAVE HIS FATHER AND MOTHER AND BE JOINED TO HIS WIFE, AND THE TWO SHALL BECOME ONE FLESH'?

6 "So they are no longer two, but one flesh. What therefore God has joined together, let no man separate."

7 They said to Him, "Why then did Moses command to GIVE HER A CERTIFICATE OF DIVORCE AND SEND her AWAY?"

8 He said to them, "Because of your hardness of heart Moses permitted you to divorce your wives; but from the beginning it has not been this way.

9 "And I say to you, whoever divorces his wife, except for immorality, and marries another woman commits adultery."

10 The disciples said to Him, "If the relationship of the man with his wife is like this, it is better not to marry."

11 But He said to them, "Not all men *can* accept this statement, but only those to whom it has been given.

12 "For there are eunuchs who were born that way from their mother's womb; and there are eunuchs who were made eunuchs by men; and there are also eunuchs who made themselves eunuchs for the sake of the kingdom of heaven. He who is able to accept this, let him accept it.

Romans 7:2-3

2 For the married woman is bound by law to her husband while he is living; but if her husband dies, she is released from the law concerning the husband.

3 So then, if while her husband is living she is joined to another man, she shall be called an adulteress; but if her husband dies, she is free from the law, so that she is not an adulteress though she is joined to another man.

1 Corinthians 6:16

16 Or do you not know that the one who joins himself to a prostitute is one body with her? For He says, "THE TWO SHALL BECOME ONE FLESH."

PROGRAM 8

The Fruit of Disobedience

TODAY'S TEXTS

Genesis 3:6-16

CROSS-REFERENCES

John 6:5-6

Psalm 22:1

Habakkuk 1:13

Genesis 4:7b

Song of Solomon 7:10

INTRODUCTION

We stop and we forget, "Hey, I'm a sinner and I'm self-centered. I'm married to a sinner. And the sinner is self-centered." And we've got to overcome the sin factor. How do we overcome the sin factor? What do we do? Well that's what this series is all about. This series is all about marriage. But, it all goes back to: what does God have to say?

QUESTIONS

1. Re-read Genesis 3:6-16 marking **man**, **woman,** and respective synonyms (e.g. husband)—but not pronouns—with different stick figures.

   a. What happened to the man and woman after they ate the fruit from the tree of the knowledge of good and evil?

   b. What did they know?

   c. What did they do?

   d. What did they hear subsequently? Who was this?

   e. What did they do in response to this "sound"?

   f. "Where" was the man? Did the Lord know? If so, why did He ask a question like this? What kind of question is this? (See **Cross-reference** John 6:5-6.)

   g. How does the man respond to the Lord? Was he "hiding" behind the fig leave coverings (3:7) or behind something else like a bush?

   h. Were the man and woman able to hide from God *successfully*?

i. What does the Lord connect the nakedness and hiding with according to v. 11?

j. What two punishments did the Lord mete out to the woman?

k. Compare the terms and structures of 3:16c and **Cross-reference** 4:7b.
   1) What term do they have in common?

   2) How does the Cross-reference help us understand the use of the term in 3:16c and therefore the meaning of 3:16?

l. Read **Cross-references** Psalm 22:1 and Habakkuk 1:13.
   1) According to the Psalm, can God "look upon" evil?

   2) According to the Prophet, in one sense can He or can He not look upon evil?

Prayer

Father, it is so difficult to submit to anyone when there are conflicts. I know I have my desires and other people have theirs. Sometimes mine are weak, other times very strong. Sometimes they're intensely personal and valuable because I have "vested interests" in certain objects and goals and so my desires are stubbornly inflexible. At other times when I could care less they're arbitrary, arrogant, and demonically irrational. Since I can't always tell the difference and can easily be deceived by the world, the devil, and my own flesh, please minimally cause me to restrain my bad attitudes and behaviors. Make me quick to hear, slow to speak, and slow to anger. Cause me to season my words always with your precious grace. Then with your Spirit help me to be genuinely humble, honoring others higher than myself—both my peers and those in authority over me. I believe You placed people in authority over me and everyone else near me for my own good—to conform me to the image of Your Son. In Jesus' name I ask for these things, Amen!

Today's Texts

Genesis 3:6-16

6 When the woman saw that the tree was good for food, and that it was a delight to the eyes, and that the tree was desirable to make one wise, she took from its fruit and ate; and she gave also to her husband with her, and he ate.

7 Then the eyes of both of them were opened, and they knew that they were naked; and they sewed fig leaves together and made themselves loin coverings.

8 They heard the sound of the LORD God walking in the garden in the cool of the day, and the man and his wife hid themselves from the presence of the LORD God among the trees of the garden.

9 Then the LORD God called to the man, and said to him, "Where are you?"

10 He said, "I heard the sound of You in the garden, and I was afraid because I was naked; so I hid myself."

11 And He said, "Who told you that you were naked? Have you eaten from the tree of which I commanded you not to eat?"

12 The man said, "The woman whom You gave to be with me, she gave me from the tree, and I ate."

13 Then the LORD God said to the woman, "What is this you have done?" And the woman said, "The serpent deceived me, and I ate."

14 The LORD God said to the serpent, "Because you have done this, cursed are you more than all cattle, and more than every beast of the field; on your belly you will go, and dust you will eat all the days of your life;

15 And I will put enmity between you and the woman, and between your seed and her seed; He shall bruise you on the head, and you shall bruise him on the heel."

16 To the woman He said, "I will greatly multiply Your pain in childbirth, in pain you will bring forth children; yet your desire will be for your husband, and he will rule over you."

John 6:5-6

5 Therefore Jesus, lifting up His eyes and seeing that a large crowd was coming to Him, said to Philip, "Where are we to buy bread, so that these may eat?"

6 This He was saying to test him, for He Himself knew what He was intending to do.

Habakkuk 1:13

13 Your eyes are too pure to approve evil, and You cannot look on wickedness *with favor*. Why do You look with favor On those who deal treacherously? Why are You silent when the wicked swallow up those more righteous than they?

Psalm 22:1

1 For the choir director; upon Aijeleth Hashshahar. A Psalm of David. My God, my God, why have You forsaken me? Far from my deliverance are the words of my groaning.

Genesis 4:7

7 "If you do well, will not *your countenance* be lifted up? And if you do not do well, sin is crouching at the door; and its desire is for you, but you must master it."

Song of Solomon 7:10

10 "I am my beloved's, and his desire is for me."

Why Happiness Eludes the Modern Woman

PROGRAM 9

TODAY'S TEXTS
Genesis 3:1-5, 14, 22
Titus 2:3-5

CROSS-REFERENCES
2 Corinthians 11:3
Revelation 12:9
John 8:44
Mark 8:33; 1:13; 4:15
Luke 13:16
2 Thessalonians 2:9
1 Corinthians 7:5
2 Corinthians 11:14

INTRODUCTION

What do you and I need to know as women? We need to know that as women, that we are called to one man, to one husband. And therefore we need to put out and shut out any thought that includes another man or causes us to look at our husband and look down our proboscis, look down our nose at our husband.

QUESTIONS

1. Re-read Genesis 3:1-5, 14, 22 marking the **devil** and all synonyms and pronouns with a red pitchfork.

   a. Who speaks to the woman in these verses?

   1) What is he called in 3:1? (Cf. v. 14.)

   2) What do we know about his identity from

   2 Corinthians 11:3?

   Revelation 12:9?

   3) What do we know about his moral characteristics from John 8:44?

   4) What do we know about his thoughts and intentions from Mark 8:33?

   5) What do we know about his actions from
   Mark 1:13?

   Mark 4:15?

   Luke 13:16?

   2 Thessalonians 2:9?

6) What do we learn about *how* he works from

    1 Corinthians 7:5?

    2 Corinthians 11:14?

b. According to Genesis 3:4, what did he tell Eve?

c. What else did he tell her according to verse 5? What this true? (See 3:22.)

d. Does the "for" that begins verse 5 explain why verse 4 is true and therefore God's original threat is false according to Satan?

e. Are Satan's lies "anything to fool with"?

2. Now review Titus 2:3-5 underlining all good characteristics of godly women. List them here. What primary purpose for these qualities does Paul have in mind?

Prayer

Father, thank you for wisdom to recognize the devil and his ways. I know he has malevolent intentions and is a liar and murderer from the very beginning of our history on earth. He's corrupt in his thinking, motives, and actions and his methods are cunning. I know he's the arch-Deceiver who appears even as an angel of light to true believers. Lord, I need not only wisdom but also your supernatural power to resist this great enemy of Your Son's Church. Among your precious promises I believe that if I "resist the devil . . . he will flee from [me]" (James 4:7). Help me resist at all costs just as Jesus did when he was tempted by overwhelming physical and spiritual needs. Cause me to seek and adopt godly thinking and behavior. In Jesus' mighty name I pray, Amen!

Today's Texts

Genesis 3:1-5, 14, 22

1 Now the serpent was more crafty than any beast of the field which the LORD God had made. And he said to the woman, "Indeed, has God said, 'You shall not eat from any tree of the garden'?"

2 The woman said to the serpent, "From the fruit of the trees of the garden we may eat;

3 but from the fruit of the tree which is in the middle of the garden, God has said, 'You shall not eat from it or touch it, or you will die.'"

4 The serpent said to the woman, "You surely will not die!

5 "For God knows that in the day you eat from it your eyes will be opened, and you will be like God, knowing good and evil."

14 The LORD God said to the serpent, "Because you have done this, cursed are you more than all cattle, and more than every beast of the field; on your belly you will go, and dust you will eat all the days of your life;

22 Then the LORD God said, "Behold, the man has become like one of us, knowing good and evil; and now, he might stretch out his hand, and take also from the tree of life, and eat, and live forever "

Titus 2:3-5

3 Older women likewise are to be reverent in their behavior, not malicious gossips nor enslaved to much wine, teaching what is good,

4 so that they may encourage the young women to love their husbands, to love their children,

5 to be sensible, pure, workers at home, kind, being subject to their own husbands, so that the word of God will not be dishonored.

2 Corinthians 11:3

3 But I am afraid that, as the serpent deceived Eve by his craftiness, your minds will be led astray from the simplicity and purity *of devotion* to Christ.

Revelation 12:9

9 And the great dragon was thrown down, the serpent of old who is called the devil and Satan, who deceives the whole world; he was thrown down to the earth, and his angels were thrown down with him.

John 8:44

44 "You are of *your* father the devil, and you want to do the desires of your father. He was a murderer from the beginning, and does not stand in the truth because there is no truth in him. Whenever he speaks a lie, he speaks from his own *nature,* for he is a liar and the father of lies.

Mark 8:33; 1:13; 4:15

33 But turning around and seeing His disciples, He rebuked Peter and said, "Get behind Me, Satan; for you are not setting your mind on God's interests, but man's."

13 And He was in the wilderness forty days being tempted by Satan; and He was with the wild beasts, and the angels were ministering to Him.

15 "These are the ones who are beside the road where the word is sown; and when they hear, immediately Satan comes and takes away the word which has been sown in them."

Luke 13:16

16 "And this woman, a daughter of Abraham as she is, whom Satan has bound for eighteen long years, should she not have been released from this bond on the Sabbath day?"

2 Thessalonians 2:9

9 *that is,* the one whose coming is in accord with the activity of Satan, with all power and signs and false wonders,

1 Corinthians 7:5

6 Stop depriving one another, except by agreement for a time, so that you may devote yourselves to prayer, and come together again so that Satan will not tempt you because of your lack of self-control.

2 Corinthians 11:14

14 No wonder, for even Satan disguises himself as an angel of light.

How To Be An Excellent Wife

PROGRAM **10**

TODAY'S TEXTS
Proverbs 31:10-31

INTRODUCTION

An excellent wife, who can find one? Son, if you find an excellent wife, you've got a woman who's worth is far above the price of all sorts of jewels. In other words she's not going to compromise. She's going to have absolutes. She's going to have a right and she's going to have a wrong. And she's going to do what's right. She's a woman of strong moral fiber.

QUESTIONS

Read Proverbs 31:10-31. List all the features of the "excellent wife" by Virtue (e.g. "trustworthy" in v. 11) and Action (e.g. "works with her hands" in v. 13 but notice that "in delight" is a virtue). Some of these will be derivative: for example a woman who rises early to work and works hard has the virtue "industrious."

Virtues	**Actions**

Prayer

Father, make me an excellent wife. In Jesus name I pray, Amen!

Today's Texts

Proverbs 31:10-31

10 An excellent wife, who can find? For her worth is far above jewels.

11 The heart of her husband trusts in her, and he will have no lack of gain.

12 She does him good and not evil all the days of her life.

13 She looks for wool and flax and works with her hands in delight.

14 She is like merchant ships; she brings her food from afar.

15 She rises also while it is still night and gives food to her household and portions to her maidens.

16 She considers a field and buys it; from her earnings she plants a vineyard.

17 She girds herself with strength and makes her arms strong.

18 She senses that her gain is good; her lamp does not go out at night.

19 She stretches out her hands to the distaff, and her hands grasp the spindle.

20 She extends her hand to the poor, and she stretches out her hands to the needy.

21 She is not afraid of the snow for her household, for all her household are clothed with scarlet.

22 She makes coverings for herself; her clothing is fine linen and purple.

23 Her husband is known in the gates, When he sits among the elders of the land.

24 She makes linen garments and sells *them,* and supplies belts to the tradesmen.

25 Strength and dignity are her clothing, and she smiles at the future.

26 She opens her mouth in wisdom, and the teaching of kindness is on her tongue.

27 She looks well to the ways of her household, and does not eat the bread of idleness.

28 Her children rise up and bless her; her husband *also,* and he praises her, *saying:*

29 "Many daughters have done nobly, *but* you excel them all."

30 Charm is deceitful and beauty is vain, but a woman who fears the LORD, she shall be praised.

31 Give her the product of her hands, and let her works praise her in the gates.

Older Women, Younger Women, Widows

PROGRAM 11

TODAY'S TEXTS
1 Timothy 5:1-16

INTRODUCTION

L adies, the way to have a marriage that runs in such a way that it's a joy to both of you is for you not to run the show. It's for you to be subject to your husband. Now, he values you as a mate. He looks at you. He respects your wisdom. He respects your gifts, and you operate together in the light of them, but when it comes right down to the fact that there can't be two heads in that household, that there has to be one, there is a time when a woman is to subject herself to her husband.

QUESTIONS

1. Read 1 Timothy 5:1-3 underlining **_widow_** and shading **_godly qualities/ actions_** for widows one color and **_ungodly qualities/actions_** another (your choice).

   According to verses 1-3 how are believers generally supposed to treat

   a. Older men?

   b. Younger men?

   c. Older women?

   d. Younger women

   e. Widows?

2. Now read 5:4-16 repeating the marking/shading above.

   a. Who is responsible for caring for parents according to

      1) Verse 4? Do verse 5's "indeed" and "alone" explain verse 4 further?

      2) Verse 8?

      3) Verse 16?

b. List the characteristic(s) of

1) the godly widow specified in verse 5:

2) the ungodly widow specified in verse 6:

c. What are Paul's two assessments of children who do not provide for their own household according to verse 8? Who does he have in mind for "household" in the context?

d. List the criteria for a widow being put on a church's "list":

e. What does Paul expect from "younger widows" that disqualify them from "listing" according to verses 11-13?

f. What does he prefer for younger widows according to verse 14 and why per 15?

g. What should a believing woman do for her "dependent widows" (e.g. her mother and mother-in-law if both living)? Do you think the plural "widows" includes a widowed daughter?

Prayer

Father, thank you for giving us wisdom concerning how to treat various kinds of widows, for revealing a clear line between personal and church responsibilities for dependents, and for telling us personally how to live out our later years if we lose our spouses. I'm so grateful for your high valuation of continuing in prayer night and day. I know I can do this ministry no matter how old or sick I get. Strengthen my spirit to continue in prayer for, and to forgive, others as Jesus did from His very cross. In his name I pray, Amen.

Today's Texts

1 Timothy 5:1-16

1 Do not sharply rebuke an older man, but *rather* appeal to *him* as a father, *to* the younger men as brothers,

2 the older women as mothers, *and* the younger women as sisters, in all purity.

3 Honor widows who are widows indeed;

4 but if any widow has children or grandchildren, they must first learn to practice piety in regard to their own family and to make some return to their parents; for this is acceptable in the sight of God.

5 Now she who is a widow indeed and who has been left alone, has fixed her hope on God and continues in entreaties and prayers night and day.

6 But she who gives herself to wanton pleasure is dead even while she lives.

7 Prescribe these things as well, so that they may be above reproach.

8 But if anyone does not provide for his own, and especially for those of his household, he has denied the faith and is worse than an unbeliever.

9 A widow is to be put on the list only if she is not less than sixty years old, *having been* the wife of one man,

10 having a reputation for good works; and if she has brought up children, if she has shown hospitality to strangers, if she has washed the saints' feet, if she has assisted those in distress, and if she has devoted herself to every good work.

11 But refuse to put younger widows on the list, for when they feel sensual desires in disregard of Christ, they want to get married,

12 thus incurring condemnation, because they have set aside their previous pledge.

13 At the same time they also learn to be idle, as they go around from house to house; and not merely idle, but also gossips and busybodies, talking about things not proper to mention.

14 Therefore, I want younger widows to get married, bear children, keep house, and give the enemy no occasion for reproach;

15 for some have already turned aside to follow Satan.

16 If any woman who is a believer has dependent widows, she must assist them and the church must not be burdened, so that it may assist those who are widows indeed.

PROGRAM 12

What God Says About A Model Man

TODAY'S TEXTS

Genesis 1:26, 28

Daniel 4:35

1 Corinthixans 11:3

John 3:16

Ephesians 5:25

Philippians 4:19

1 Timothy 5:8; 3:1-13

Titus 1:5-9

INTRODUCTION

Pardon me, darling, but are you looking for a man? And what kind of a man are you looking for? What is your model man, the kind of man that you've dreamed of, the kind of man that you want to be married to? Or excuse me, sir. Do you have a model that you can follow? Do you have an example of all that a man should be? We're going to look at what God says a model man is.

QUESTIONS

1. Read the following pairs of scriptures, then for each: title the role man plays in a marriage that reflects God's attribute.

   a. _____ Genesis 1:26, 28

   b. _____ Daniel 4:35; 1 Corinthians 11:3

   c. _____ John 3:16; Ephesians 5:25

   d. _____ Philippians 4:19; 1 Timothy 5:8

2. Now read 1 Timothy 3:1-13 and Titus 1:5-9 and list in the columns below the criteria for male leaders (elders and deacons) in the church. Try to list identical and similar criteria on the same line (in parallel):

1 Timothy 3:1-13	Titus 1:5-9

Prayer

Prayer for the single woman: *Father, I know how easy it is to be attracted to the wrong things—money, good looks, strength, status. Help me resist these biological, financial, and social factors and seek a godly man for marriage. Lead him to me and cause me to see these inner qualities and not be distracted by the rest. Until that time, Lord, I'm your faithful servant. Help me produce spiritual children for your kingdom.*

Prayer for the man: *Lord, I want to be a godly model wherever you lead me. I can't be all these many qualities Paul lists without your power. Even if I can manage some of them from day to day, I can't sustain them without your ongoing power. Strengthen and sustain me, Lord—to be a great leader in my church and in my marriage.*

In Jesus name, Amen!

Today's Texts

Genesis 1:26, 28

26 Then God said, "Let Us make man in Our image, according to Our likeness; and let them rule over the fish of the sea and over the birds of the sky and over the cattle and over all the earth, and over every creeping thing that creeps on the earth."

28 God blessed them; and God said to them, "Be fruitful and multiply, and fill the earth, and subdue it; and rule over the fish of the sea and over the birds of the sky and over every living thing that moves on the earth."

Daniel 4:35

35 "All the inhabitants of the earth are accounted as nothing, but He does according to His will in the host of heaven and *among* the inhabitants of earth; and no one can ward off His hand Or say to Him, 'What have You done?' "

1 Corinthians 11:3

3 But I want you to understand that Christ is the head of every man, and the man is the head of a woman, and God is the head of Christ.

John 3:16

16 "For God so loved the world, that He gave His only begotten Son, that whoever believes in Him shall not perish, but have eternal life."

Ephesians 5:25

25 Husbands, love your wives, just as Christ also loved the church and gave Himself up for her,

Philippians 4:19

19 And my God will supply all your needs according to His riches in glory in Christ Jesus.

1 Timothy 5:8

8 But if anyone does not provide for his own, and especially for those of his household, he has denied the faith and is worse than an unbeliever.

1 Timothy 3:1-13

1 It is a trustworthy statement: if any man aspires to the office of overseer, it is a fine work he desires to do.

2 An overseer, then, must be above reproach, the husband of one wife, temperate, prudent, respectable, hospitable, able to teach,

3 not addicted to wine or pugnacious, but gentle, peaceable, free from the love of money.

4 He must be one who manages his own household well, keeping his children under control with all dignity

5 (but if a man does not know how to manage his own household, how will he take care of the church of God?),

6 and not a new convert, so that he will not become conceited and fall into the condemnation incurred by the devil.

7 And he must have a good reputation with those outside the church, so that he will not fall into reproach and the snare of the devil.

8 Deacons likewise must be men of dignity, not double-tongued, or addicted to much wine or fond of sordid gain,

9 but holding to the mystery of the faith with a clear conscience.

10 These men must also first be tested; then let them serve as deacons if they are beyond reproach.

11 Women *must* likewise *be* dignified, not malicious gossips, but temperate, faithful in all things.

12 Deacons must be husbands of *only* one wife, *and* good managers of *their* children and their own households.

13 For those who have served well as deacons obtain for themselves a high standing and great confidence in the faith that is in Christ Jesus.

Titus 1:5-9

5 For this reason I left you in Crete, that you would set in order what remains and appoint elders in every city as I directed you,

6 *namely,* if any man is above reproach, the husband of one wife, having children who believe, not accused of dissipation or rebellion.

7 For the overseer must be above reproach as God's steward, not self-willed, not quick-tempered, not addicted to wine, not pugnacious, not fond of sordid gain,

8 but hospitable, loving what is good, sensible, just, devout, self-controlled,

9 holding fast the faithful word which is in accordance with the teaching, so that he will be able both to exhort in sound doctrine and to refute those who contradict.

How To Be The Man You Want To Be

PROGRAM 13

TODAY'S TEXTS
1 Timothy 3:2-4

INTRODUCTION

One of the things God expects if you become a father is that the father is to bring the child up in the nurture and admonition of the Lord. And that word "admonition" (of the Lord) means instruction. You're to discipline them. You're to child train them. And that child training implies that there is some instruction there. So although you may not be a platform speaker, you're a man who knows truth.

CROSS-REFERENCES
Ecclesiastes 3:1-8

Philippians 3:12

1 Timothy 5:10

Hebrews 13:2

Ephesians 6:4

Deuteronomy 6:7

QUESTIONS

Read 1 Timothy 3:2-4. Review and fill in the qualifications for an overseer in the blank lines, then write in some illustrations to show what this "looks like" in real life.

1. _____This quality implies that "there's nothing in the man you can use against him." Does this mean absolutely sinless?

DID YOU KNOW?
μιᾶς γυναικὸς ἄνδρα (*mias yunaikos andra:* 1 Timothy 3:2) translated "the husband of one wife" but literally "a one-woman male."

φιλοξενιας (*philoxenias:* Hebrews 13:2) from *phileo*, to love, and *xenos*, stranger.

2. _____This quality means complete physical, mental, spiritual commitment to a wife. (See **Did You Know?**)

3. _____ This quality means "doesn't fly off the handle," not erratic but "even keeled."

4. _____ This quality means "when to do what"—how to behave wisely in all circumstances (see **Cross-reference** Ecclesiastes 3:1-8). It's a progressive quality (see **Cross-reference** Philippians 3:12).

5. _____ This quality means kindness to strangers (See **Cross-references** 1 Timothy 5:10 and Hebrews 13:2 and **Did You Know?**)

6. _____ This quality means doctrinally sound, not necessarily a passionate speaker.

7. _____ This quality means self-controlled with respect to wine.

8. _____ This quality relates to "Let's fight!"

9. _____ This quality is the opposite of "Let's fight!"

10. _____ This quality relates to "the root of all evil."

11. _____ This quality relates to managing one's household, not provoking children to wrath (See **Cross-references** Ephesians 6:4 and Deuteronomy 6:7.)

Prayer

Father, I want to be Your man, the true man, the ideal man; I want to be just like Jesus, perfect in every way. I realize now from Your Word just how many qualities this entails. They are all impossible without Your Spirit working them in me. So please Lord, I ask you to work these qualities in my spirit and soul and body continuously . . . until I am "complete, without blame at the coming of our Lord Jesus Christ" (1 Thessalonians 5:23), Your only Son. Amen!

Today's Texts

1 Timothy 3:2-4

2 An overseer, then, must be above reproach, the husband of one wife, temperate, prudent, respectable, hospitable, able to teach,

3 not addicted to wine or pugnacious, but gentle, peaceable, free from the love of money.

4 He must be one who manages his own household well, keeping his children under control with all dignity

Ecclesiastes 3:1-8

1 There is an appointed time for everything. And there is a time for every event under heaven—

2 A time to give birth and a time to die; a time to plant and a time to uproot what is planted.

3 time to kill and a time to heal; a time to tear down and a time to build up.

4 time to weep and a time to laugh; a time to mourn and a time to dance.

5 time to throw stones and a time to gather stones; a time to embrace and a time to shun embracing.

6 time to search and a time to give up as lost; a time to keep and a time to throw away.

7 time to tear apart and a time to sew together; a time to be silent and a time to speak.

8 A time to love and a time to hate; a time for war and a time for peace.

Philippians 3:12

12 Not that I have already obtained *it* or have already become perfect, but I press on so that I may lay hold of that for which also I was laid hold of by Christ Jesus.

1 Timothy 5:10

10 having a reputation for good works; *and* if she has brought up children, if she has shown hospitality to strangers, if she has washed the saints' feet, if she has assisted those in distress, and if she has devoted herself to every good work.

Hebrews 13:2

2 Do not neglect to show hospitality to strangers, for by this some have entertained angels without knowing it.

Ephesians 6:4

4 Fathers, do not provoke your children to anger, but bring them up in the discipline and instruction of the Lord.

Deuteronomy 6:7

7 You shall teach them diligently to your sons and shall talk of them when you sit in your house and when you walk by the way and when you lie down and when you rise up.

PROGRAM 14

Contrast A Model Man and An Evil Man

TODAY'S TEXTS
Titus 1:5-9, 12

2 Timothy 3:1-2

CROSS-REFERENCES
Isaiah 1:2-4

Titus 1:12

Joshua 1:8

2 Timothy 4:7-8

1 Corinthians 11:1

DID YOU KNOW?
τεκνα ἔχων πιστά, μη κὰτηγορίᾳ ἀσωτίας ἤ ἀνυπότακτα. (Titus 1:6: *tekna echon pista, me en kategoria asotias e anupotakta*), literally "children having faith, not in accusation of dissipation or rebellion."

The NAU and ESV read *pista* "believers" *in terms of assent to Christian doctrine* (the faith). The KJV reads it "faithful" *in terms of moral behavior* (trustworthy, dependable) possibly relative "to parents" based on the two *qualifying* terms that immediately follow (in Greek word order, see underlining at the top): "faithful—not *publicly* accusable of dissipation or rebellion."

What do you think and why? Can you find other scriptures that relate to the interpretation of this important qualification for leaders?

INTRODUCTION

Jesus is coming again. And when He comes again, the second time, He's coming for judgment. When He comes the second time, He's coming to take over. I mean, He is saying, "Move over all you leaders. Move over all you nations. I'm here and I am God and I've come to take over." He's going to judge all those that have mistreated His people. There is a payday, someday. And it is coming.

QUESTIONS

1. Read Titus 1:5-9, 12.

    a. Why did Paul leave Timothy in Crete?

    b. What were Cretans like per verse 12? List three of their characteristics:

    c. What primary characteristic for a leader heads the list in verse 5?

    d. A leader's children:

    1) Positive characteristic (See **Did You Know?**) _____

    2) Negative characteristics to avoid:

    _____

    _____

    e. A leader's "drinking habits": _____

    f. A leader's attitude toward possessions: _____

    g. A leader's attitude toward strangers: _____

    h. What three qualities do leaders "love"?

    1) _____

    2) _____

    3) _____

i. A leader's spiritual life and temperament?

j. A leader's relationship to the Word of God? (See **Cross-reference** Joshua 1:8)

2. According to 2 Timothy 4:7-8:

   a. What has Paul done? What did this include according to Cross-reference 1 Corinthians 11:1?

   b. What is "laid up" for him?

   c. What characterizes those whom it is "laid up" for?

   d. What will Jesus do when He returns?

3. Now read 2 Timothy 3:1-2. List the characteristics of the wicked in "the last days."

   a. _____ ‹ who the wicked will love

   b. _____ ‹ what the wicked will love

   c. _____ ‹ a general verbal action toward others

   d. _____ ‹ the general attitude that fuels 3 (prior question).

   e. _____ ‹ an action that demeans others

   f. _____ ‹ action related to parents

   g. _____ ‹ attitude related to people who have given them things

   h. _____ ‹ spiritual condition related to one of God's attributes

Prayer

Father, thank you for clearly contrasting the Model Man and the Evil Man of the last days. They are so opposed; I can see why the wicked are hostile to those who know You intimately. Lord, please give me power to live a godly life to be a godly example to my family, friends, coworkers, and even strangers. I want my life to influence others to receive Jesus and His salvation. In His name I pray, Amen.

Today's Texts

Titus 1:5-9, 12

5 For this reason I left you in Crete, that you would set in order what remains and appoint elders in every city as I directed you,

6 namely, if any man is above reproach, the husband of one wife, having children who believe, not accused of dissipation or rebellion.

7 For the overseer must be above reproach as God's steward, not self-willed, not quick-tempered, not addicted to wine, not pugnacious, not fond of sordid gain,

8 but hospitable, loving what is good, sensible, just, devout, self-controlled,

9 holding fast the faithful word which is in accordance with the teaching, so that he will be able both to exhort in sound doctrine and to refute those who contradict.

12 One of themselves, a prophet of their own, said, "Cretans are always liars, evil beasts, lazy gluttons."

2 Timothy 3:1-2

1 But realize this, that in the last days difficult times will come.

2 For men will be lovers of self, lovers of money, boastful, arrogant, revilers, disobedient to parents, ungrateful, unholy,

Isaiah 1:2-4

2 Listen, O heavens, and hear, O earth; For the LORD speaks, "Sons I have reared and brought up, but they have revolted against Me.

3 An ox knows its owner, And a donkey its master's manger, but Israel does not know, My people do not understand."

4 Alas, sinful nation, People weighed down with iniquity, Offspring of evildoers, Sons who act corruptly! They have abandoned the LORD, they have despised the Holy One of Israel, they have turned away from Him.

Titus 1:12

12 One of themselves, a prophet of their own, said, "Cretans are always liars, evil beasts, lazy gluttons."

Joshua 1:8

8 "This book of the law shall not depart from your mouth, but you shall meditate on it day and night, so that you may be careful to do according to all that is written in it; for then you will make your way prosperous, and then you will have success."

2 Timothy 4:7-8

7 have fought the good fight, I have finished the course, I have kept the faith;

8 in the future there is laid up for me the crown of righteousness, which the Lord, the righteous Judge, will award to me on that day; and not only to me, but also to all who have loved His appearing.

1 Corinthians 11:1

1 Be imitators of me, just as I also am of Christ.

Four Different Kinds of Love

PROGRAM **15**

TODAY'S TEXTS

Romans 1:31
2 Timothy 3:3
Proverbs 30:16 (LXX)
Luke 7:6
Luke 20:46
John 5:20
John 11:11
John 15:14-15
Matthew 5:46
Luke 11:43
John 3:16
John 3:35

INTRODUCTION

Can you imagine what would happen in homes all over if, when the two mates got together either when they both came home from work or when the husband came home and found the wife at home, and she would just say, "I am so glad to see you. I've missed you. You are so wonderful. You are such an awesome man. You know today, I was just thinking about you and I was just thinking how blessed I am to have a husband like you!!"? Do you realize what that would do for the man?

QUESTIONS

The Four Loves

1. στοργη (*storge*). Read **Did You Know?** and then the following verses. Write in the English term each of the four translations uses. Then check the context to discover the terms this adjective is associated with.

    a. Romans 1:31 (The negative **astorgos** = *not-storge*, the 3rd term in the verse)

    NASB

    ESV

    KJV

    RSV

    <u>Associated with:</u>

DID YOU KNOW?

"Observe how complex is a parental love [φιλοτεκνίας] affection [στοργὴ: *storge*] for her children, which draws everything toward an emotion felt in her inmost parts" (4 Maccabbees 14:13). We're citing the Septuagint Greek (LXX) version of this apocryphal book *only* to show the only one of two verses we can find the use of the positive term. (The other verse is 14:17.)

The references we cite in the questions use the negative term **astorgos** = *not storge*.

    b. 2 Timothy 3:3 (The negative again, here the 1st term in the verse)
    NASB

    ESV

    KJV

    RSV

    <u>Associated with:</u>

2. ἔρως *(eros)*. This term is found only in the Septuagint (LXX) version of Proverbs 30:16 which speaks of the "*eros* of a woman" as something that, among the other things listed, is "never satisfied." The term is used extensively in other Greek writings from Homer forward. We derive our English word erotic from this Greek term so you can pretty much guess what's in mind.

3. φιλος *(philos)*. Read the following verses to discover the English term that most frequently translates this "love" term which is often found in compound form in Greek and English: *philosophy* (love of wisdom), *philadelphia* (love of brethren), etc.

   a. Luke 7:6

   b. Luke 20:46

   c. John 5:20

   d. John 11:11

   e. John 15:14-15

   Meaning:

4. ἀγάπη *(agape)*. We'll be studying this extensively next week. For now, read the following verses and see if you can determine the meaning of this frequently used Greek term for "love":

   a. Matthew 5:46

   b. Luke 11:43 (compare with 20:46 above)

   c. John 3:16

   d. John 3:35 (compare with 5:20 above)

   Meaning:

Prayer

Father, I am fascinated by these four kinds of love but discouraged by how far I fall short of all of them. Lord, give me a heart to love You, my family at home, my friends at church, and everyone else You put within my reach. Help me love as Jesus loved; turn me away from every thought, choice, and action that are not characterized by love. Cause me to love those who are easy to love and those who are not. I want to do all these things to and for Your glory. In the name of Jesus I pray, Amen!

Today's Texts

Romans 1:31

31 without understanding, untrustworthy, unloving [*astorgous*], unmerciful;

2 Timothy 3:3

3 Unloving [*astorgoi*], irreconcilable, malicious gossips, without self-control, brutal, haters of good,

LXX Proverbs 30:16

16 Hades, and an erotic [*eros*] woman, and Tartaros, and earth not satisfied with water, and water and fire which never say "Enough!"

Luke 7:6

6 Now Jesus started on His way with them; and when He was not far from the house, the centurion sent friends [*philous*], saying to Him, "Lord, do not trouble Yourself further, for I am not worthy for You to come under my roof;"

Luke 20:46

46 "Beware of the scribes, who like to walk around in long robes, and love [*philounton*] respectful greetings in the market places, and chief seats in the synagogues and places of honor at banquets,

John 5:20

20 "For the Father loves [*philei*] the Son, and shows Him all things that He Himself is doing; and *the Father* will show Him greater works than these, so that you will marvel."

John 11:11

11 This He said, and after that He said to them, "Our friend [*philos*] Lazarus has fallen asleep; but I go, so that I may awaken him out of sleep."

John 15:14-15

14 "You are My friends [*philoi*] if you do what I command you.

15 "No longer do I call you slaves, for the slave does not know what his master is doing; but I have called you friends [*philous*], for all things that I have heard from My Father I have made known to you."

Matthew 5:46

46 "For if you love [*agapesete*] those who love [*agapontas*] you, what reward do you have? Do not even the tax collectors do the same?"

Luke 11:43

10 "Woe to you Pharisees! For you love [*agapate*] the chief seats in the synagogues and the respectful greetings in the market places."

John 3:16

16 "For God so loved [*egapesen*] the world, that He gave His only begotten Son, that whoever believes in Him shall not perish, but have eternal life."

John 3:35

35 The Father loves [*agapa*] the Son and has given all things into His hand.

PROGRAM **16**

Unconditional Love

TODAY'S TEXTS

Jeremiah 31:3

John 3:16

1 John 4:7, 9, 10, 19

INTRODUCTION

Unconditional love, **agape** love, is a love that desires another's highest good. It is a love that is focused toward the object of that love. "Love is from God . . . . the one who does not love does not know God, for God is love" (1 John 4:7, 8). God is *agape*. He is unconditional, sacrificial, everlasting, ministering love.

DID YOU KNOW?

The Septuagint (LXX) was the first Greek translation of the OT Scriptures. You'll note in Today's Texts that we included the LXX's translation of the Hebrew אֲהַבַת (*ahavat*) by ἠγάπησά (*egapesa*) in Jeremiah 31:3. *Egapesa* is the aorist (simple past) tense of *agapao* which is associated with the noun *agape*.

QUESTIONS

1. Read Jeremiah 31:3, marking every noun **love** ♥ and every verb form (**love, loves, loved, loving**) with a red heart. (Note: all the verses listed in **Today's Texts** contain a tense of the Greek verb *agapao* and/or the corresponding noun *agape*).

   a. How is God's love for Israel (v. 2) characterized? How far back does it go?

   b. Explain "therefore." Are God's mind/will and actions disconnected?

2. Now read John 3:16, marking every **love** as above.

   a. Explain the first "that" in the verse. What thoughts does it connect?

   b. How does "only begotten" value God's love?

   c. How does "gave" value God's love? Was this love conditional or unconditional? If conditional, what was it conditioned on?

3. Finally, read 1 John 4:7, 9, 10, and 19, marking every **love**.

   a. What is the source of love?

   b. What is the connection between "born of God" and love?

   c. How was God's love manifested (revealed)? What did He do?

   d. Did God love us because we first loved Him?

Prayer

Father, thank You for Your unconditional, sacrificial, everlasting, ministering love. I realize that without it every man who has ever walked the earth is hopeless. Because we don't love You by nature, I am also so grateful for a new birth that enables me to love others the way You loved me. Thank you for this precious gift of regeneration I did not deserve. Please continue to fill this new nature with Your Holy Spirit so I will represent Your love to others You are willing to save. In Jesus' name, Amen!

Today's Texts

Jeremiah 31:3

3 The LORD appeared to him from afar, *saying,* "I have loved [LXX: *egapesa*] you with an everlasting [LXX: *aionian*] love [*agapesin*]; therefore I have drawn you with lovingkindness."

John 3:16

16 "For God so loved [*egapesen*] the world, that He gave His only begotten Son, that whoever believes in Him shall not perish, but have eternal life."

1 John 4:7, 9, 10, 19

7 Beloved [*Agapetoi*], let us love [*agapomen*] one another, for love [*agape*] is from God; and everyone who loves [*agapon*] is born of God and knows God.

9 By this the love [*agape*] of God was manifested in us, that God has sent His only begotten Son into the world so that we might live through Him.

10 In this is love [*agape*], not that we loved [*egapekamen*] God, but that He loved [*egapesen*] us and sent His Son to be the propitiation for our sins.

19 We love [*agapomen*], because He first loved [*egapesen*] us.

PROGRAM 17

How is Love Expressed?

TODAY'S TEXTS

Matthew 19:19

Ephesians 5:25

1 John 4:7

INTRODUCTION

You are commanded by God to love your wife as Christ loved the church. What happens when a man doesn't love his wife as Christ loved the church? What happens when he refuses to love his wife? What happens when he doesn't care for her or when he doesn't meet her needs, when he doesn't seek to make her comfortable, when he doesn't seek to show her that she is special, when he doesn't respond to her love? What happens? God judges that man.

QUESTIONS

1. Review God's general command to us to love (*agape*) one another in Matthew 19:19 and 1 John 4:7 and then His specific command to husbands to love (*agape*) their wives in Ephesians 5:25.

2. For each of Kay's four "expressions" of *agape* from her program, given below, list examples of things you can do.

Love consists in making another person feel

a. Comfortable

b. Special

c. Appreciated/praised (responding to love from others)

Prayer

Father, You commanded me to love others as myself and told me that this very love (agape) is from You. From an earlier lesson I learned from your Word that people are capable of this love only if they are born again. I know you have regenerated my heart so I thank You for this special love empowered by Your Holy Spirit. Please help me express it by the things I listed. I want my actions to match the intentions of my heart and glorify You publicly. Help me express this love to everyone You bring to me. In Jesus' name and for Your sake I pray, Amen!

Today's Texts

Matthew 19:19

19 "You shall love [*agapeseis*] your neighbor as yourself." (Note: while Jesus may have quoted from the Hebrew Scriptures, the Greek translation [Septuagint or LXX] of Leviticus 19:18 uses the same verb *agapao* and it was widely circulated in Jesus' day.)

Ephesians 5:25

25 Husbands, love [*agapate*] your wives, just as Christ also loved [*egapesen*] the church and gave Himself up for her,

1 John 4:7

7 Beloved [*Agapetoi*], let us love [*agapomen*] one another, for love [*agape*] is from God.

PROGRAM 18

TODAY'S TEXTS

Proverbs 18:21

James 3:3-12

Ephesians 4:29

Genesis 2:23-25; 3:11

CROSS-REFERENCES

Colossians 4:6

Matthew 19:6

Ephesians 5:25, 33

Essentials For Communication

INTRODUCTION

Sometimes because there's such pain in the past, and such hurt in the past, we don't understand what we're battling against in that communication. We don't understand why we say something and all of a sudden our mate goes into a rage, gets furious or just bursts out in tears or absolutely clams up. We don't understand that, because there's not an openness. And so if you're going to have a healthy communication with one another, you need to be open.

QUESTIONS

1. Read Proverbs 18:21 marking *tongue* and pronouns with a megaphone.

    a. What two fruits is the tongue capable of producing?

    b. What does "eat its fruits" mean?

    c. How do you want to use your tongue? Who should you use it for?

2. Read James 3:3-12. Continue to mark *tongue* as above.

    a. What things is the tongue compared to in this section? Even though these things are small what kind of effects do they produce per the text?

    b. What descriptions show us how powerful the tongue is? Can we tame it?

    c. How is the tongue inconsistent? Do you use your tongue inconsistently?

3. Read Ephesians 4:29 and **cross-reference** Colossians 4:6. In 4:29 mark the phrase ***word proceed from your mouth*** with a megaphone. See **Did You Know?** to the left.

DID YOU KNOW?

Edification (οἰκοδομὴν: *oikodomen*, Ephesians 4:29). This Greek noun is associated with the verb *oikodomeo*: to build a building—an edifice.

Edification, then, is associated with "building" ideas like massiveness, strength, and permanence. When you edify someone with your words you're spiritually strengthening them.

Ephesians 4:29 includes the idea of wise timing—edification for "the need" (i.e. of the moment)—and identifies these right words with "giving grace to those who hear."

The words are contrasted with "unwholesome [*sapros*: rotten] words" that rot or decay, as opposed to build up and strengthen.

a. What kind of words should we restrain?

b. What kind should we speak and when?

c. Why? What do these words do?

Four Essential Truths About Marriage that Produce Good Communication

1. **Priority.** Read Genesis 2:23-25.
   a. What's unique about the origin of the woman?

   b. What do the man and woman become in marriage? Does this condition imply the priority of the marriage relationship for communication?

2. **Permanence.** Review Genesis 2:24 and **Cross-reference** Matthew 19:6.
   a. How long is marriage for?

   b. Is a wedding a marriage? Who actually marries people, God or man?

   c. On whose authority do we have this?

3. **Oneness.** Review Genesis 2:24 and **Cross-references** Matthew 19:6, Ephesians 5:25 and 33.
   a. How does the Word define marriage in Genesis 2:24? What does "one flesh" mean?

   b. What two ways is a husband to love his wife according to the two verses in Ephesians? How does the second one contribute to the idea of unity?

      1) as _____

      2) as _____

4. **Openness.** Review Genesis 2:25 and read Genesis 3:11.
   a. What do "naked" and "unashamed" mean?

   b. Why did the man and woman become ashamed? What's the first question God asks them? The second?

   c. What does hiding nakedness imply with respect to honest and open communication?

   d. How well are you at openly communicating with your spouse? What can you improve?

Prayer

Father, I understand and believe the four essential truths about marriage from Your Word that will help me love my spouse and communicate lovingly. I believe my marriage is my highest priority among all my relationships; I believe marriage is permanent; I believe it's a union of two bodies and spirits; and I believe it's an open relationship, one of honest communication without deceit and hypocrisy. Lord, understanding the power of the tongue, cause me to restrain unwholesome words that destroy people and, as occasions arise, cause me to speak gracious words that build up and strengthen people in need. In Jesus' name, Amen!

Today's Texts

Proverbs 18:21

21 Death and life are in the power of the tongue, and those who love it will eat its fruit

James 3:3-12

3 Now if we put the bits into the horses' mouths so that they will obey us, we direct their entire body as well.

4 Look at the ships also, though they are so great and are driven by strong winds, are still directed by a very small rudder wherever the inclination of the pilot desires.

5 So also the tongue is a small part of the body, and *yet* it boasts of great things. See how great a forest is set aflame by such a small fire!

6 And the tongue is a fire, the *very* world of iniquity; the tongue is set among our members as that which defiles the entire body, and sets on fire the course of *our* life, and is set on fire by hell.

7 For every species of beasts and birds, of reptiles and creatures of the sea, is tamed and has been tamed by the human race.

8 But no one can tame the tongue; *it is* a restless evil *and* full of deadly poison.

9 With it we bless *our* Lord and Father, and with it we curse men, who have been made in the likeness of God;

10 from the same mouth come *both* blessing and cursing. My brethren, these things ought not to be this way.

11   Does a fountain send out from the same opening *both* fresh and bitter water?

12 Can a fig tree, my brethren, produce olives, or a vine produce figs? Nor *can* salt water produce fresh.

Ephesians 4:29

29 Let no unwholesome word proceed from your mouth, but only such *a word* as is good for edification according to the need *of the moment,* so that it will give grace to those who hear.

Genesis 2:23-25; 3:11

23 The man said, "This is now bone of my bones, and flesh of my flesh; she shall be called Woman, because she was taken out of Man."

24 For this reason a man shall leave his father and his mother, and be joined to his wife; and they shall become one flesh.

25 And the man and his wife were both naked and were not ashamed.

11 And He said, "Who told you that you were naked? Have you eaten from the tree of which I commanded you not to eat?"

Colossians 4:6

9 Let your speech [literally 'your word'] always be with grace, *as though* seasoned with salt, so that you will know how you should respond to each person.

Matthew 19:6

6 "So they are no longer two, but one flesh. What therefore God has joined together, let no man separate."

Ephesians 5:25, 33

25 Husbands, love your wives, just as Christ also loved the church and gave Himself up for her,

33 Nevertheless, each individual among you also is to love his own wife even as himself, and the wife must *see to it* that she respects her husband.

PROGRAM **19**

Ministry of Communication

TODAY'S TEXTS

Proverbs 17:17

Proverbs 18:21

Matthew 7:1, 2

Romans 2:1

James 4:11

Romans 12:10

James 1:19

1 John 3:18

INTRODUCTION

In Proverbs, chapter 17, verse 17: "But there's a friend that loves at all times. And a brother is born for adversity." So in this communication where you have to be careful that you don't judge them, you don't criticize them, you don't give advice too quickly and you don't figure that person out and put them in a slot and say, "You always are this way. You will never change. That's always your MO, your method of operation!"

Look, stop and just know this. If a brother is born for the day of adversity, then in this marriage situation, you need to be the friend. And you need to sit back and you need to listen and you need to keep the communication open wide.

CROSS-REFERENCES

2 Corinthians 3:7

Matthew 12:36-37

QUESTIONS

1. Read Proverbs Proverbs 18:21 and **Cross-references** 2 Corinthians 3:7 and Matthew 12:37.

   a. What two powers are in the tongue? Is there a gray or neutral area between these two? Do you think every categorical judgment we speak has either life or death attached to it?

   b. What does Paul mean by "the ministry of death" (2 Corinthians 3:7) in the context? Do legalism and its accompanying self-righteousness minister and communicate death to people? If so, how?

   c. Why are our words so significant according to Jesus in Matthew 12:36-37?

2. What attitudes should we have in our communication according to:

   a. Matthew 7:1, 2?

   b. Romans 2:1?

   c. James 4:11?

3. Generally, what does Paul counsel us to do according to the second part of Romans 12:10? How does this bear on communication?

4. List James' three exhortations in James 1:19, note how each improves communication, write out what you plan to do with each tomorrow and who you think will be most impacted.

   a. Quick to _____

   b. Slow to _____

   c. Slow to _____

5. Read 1 John 3:18.
   a. Are there non-verbal ways of loving?

   b. List some practical ways you can do these "way"s.

6. What practical instructions for good communication do we get from:
   a. Proverbs 18:13?

   b. Proverbs 15:2?

   c. Proverbs 29:20?

7. How can you apply these today? Who do you think needs you to communicate these ways the most?

8. If sometime you want do a long but productive inductive Bible study, go through Proverbs shading every good communication with the tongue green and every bad one red. Then list the verse addresses and short versions of them in two columns. Pray for the Lord's power to start the green and *stop* the red.

Prayer

Father, I want to communicate life with my tongue. I realize to do this I have to preempt my words with a forgiving, non-critical spirit. I have to be quick to hear, slow to speak, and slow to anger. Then I have to season what words I do end up speaking with Your wisdom, grace, and mercy. Lord, keep careless and useless words from leaving my mouth. Help me love not in word but in deed and truth. Give me a heart of unconditional love toward all people and cause me to honor them above myself. In Jesus' name I pray, Amen!

Today's Texts

Proverbs 17:17

17 A friend loves at all times, and a brother is born for adversity.

Proverbs 18:21

21 Death and life are in the power of the tongue, And those who love it will eat its fruit.

Matthew 7:1, 2

1 "Do not judge so that you will not be judged.

2 "For in the way you judge, you will be judged; and by your standard of measure, it will be measured to you."

Romans 2:1

1 Therefore you have no excuse, every one of you who passes judgment, for in that which you judge another, you condemn yourself; for you who judge practice the same things.

James 4:11

11 Do not speak against one another, brethren. He who speaks against a brother or judges his brother, speaks against the law and judges the law; but if you judge the law, you are not a doer of the law but a judge *of it.*

Romans 12:10

10 *Be* devoted to one another in brotherly love; give preference to one another in honor;

James 1:19

19 *This* you know, my beloved brethren. But everyone must be quick to hear, slow to speak *and* slow to anger;

1 John 3:18

18 Little children, let us not love with word or with tongue, but in deed and truth.

2 Corinthians 3:7

7 But if the ministry of death, in letters engraved on stones, came with glory, so that the sons of Israel could not look intently at the face of Moses because of the glory of his face, fading *as* it was . . .

Matthew 12:36, 37

36 "But I tell you that every careless word that people speak, they shall give an accounting for it in the day of judgment.

37 "For by your words you will be justified, and by your words you will be condemned."

Art of Communication

PROGRAM 20

INTRODUCTION

One of our staff members has a son who's always felt stupid, because one day a teacher turned around in school and said, "You are stupid!" It was a lie, and you've got to know that God wants to use our tongue to bring healing. He wants to use our tongues to tell truth to people, because the devil's out there sowing all sorts of lies and he is a murderer and he is a destroyer and he is a deceiver.

Read **Today's Texts**, then complete the columns below for the two categories, Speech and Attitude. We did the first one for you.

TODAY'S TEXTS

Romans 15:7
Proverbs 15:4; 18:14
Ephesians 5:29; 4:15
2 Timothy 2:24
Proverbs 15:1; 16:21; 15:28
Colossians 4:6
Proverbs 16:24; 19:11

VERSE	GOOD TONGUE	BAD TONGUE
Proverbs 15:4	Soothing tongue—Tree of life	Perverse tongue—crushes spirit

	GOOD ATTITUDE	BAD ATTITUDE
Romans 15:7	Accepting others (praise)	Rejecting others (criticism)

Prayer

Father, thank You so much for teaching me the Art of Communication from the wisdom You have recorded and left for us in Your Word. I know that good communication starts with a good attitude that stirs up good motives. Make my heart right toward other people; fill me with acceptance and grace and mercy. Cause me to heal broken hearts and depressed spirits, there are so many around me. Help me overlook transgressions and keep me from arguing. Make my words soft and sweet so they will heal people, body and soul. I want to be a loving communicator. In Jesus' name and for Your glory I ask these things. Amen!

Today's Texts

Romans 15:7

7 Therefore, accept one another, just as Christ also accepted us to the glory of God.

Proverbs 15:4

4 A soothing tongue is a tree of life, but perversion in it crushes the spirit.

Proverbs 18:14

14 The spirit of a man can endure his sickness, but *as for* a broken spirit who can bear it?

Ephesians 5:29

29 for no one ever hated his own flesh, but nourishes and cherishes it, just as Christ also *does* the church,

Ephesians 4:15

15 but speaking the truth in love, we are to grow up in all *aspects* into Him who is the head, *even* Christ,

2 Timothy 2:24

24 The Lord's bond-servant must not be quarrelsome, but be kind to all, able to teach, patient when wronged,

Proverbs 15:1

1 A gentle answer turns away wrath, but a harsh word stirs up anger.

Proverbs 16:21

21 The wise in heart will be called understanding, and sweetness of speech increases persuasiveness.

Proverbs 15:28

28 The heart of the righteous ponders how to answer, but the mouth of the wicked pours out evil things.

Colossians 4:6

6 Let your speech always be with grace, *as though* seasoned with salt, so that you will know how you should respond to each person.

Proverbs 16:24

24 Pleasant words are a honeycomb, sweet to the soul and healing to the bones.

Proverbs 19:11

11 A man's discretion makes him slow to anger, and it is his glory to overlook a transgression.

Dorie–Unloved and Unwanted

PROGRAM 21

TODAY

Kay's guest today is Dorie N. Van Stone (1st of 3 programs).

INTRODUCTION

God had told Dorie that He loved her. He had affirmed that in the Word of God. And this treasured little Book was the thing that held her and affirmed her over and over again that He was there, that He cared for her, that she was precious in His sight. And yet, what does God do? He comes along and He puts people in her life, people that come along and confirm to her with their words that she does have significance.

Enjoy Kay's interview of Dorie N. Van Stone, author of *No Place to Cry: The Hurt and Healing of Sexual Abuse* and *Dorie: The Girl Nobody Loved.*

PROGRAM 22

Importance Of Our Words

TODAY

Kay's guest today is Dorie N. Van Stone (2nd of 3 programs).

How are you cleansed? You're cleansed through the washing of the water of the Word of God. You can become a brand-new creature in Christ Jesus. And old things can pass away and all things can become new. Find out how to have life and how to know the love of God that will hold you and transform you and keep you and will never leave you and never forsake you. You are precious to God. Let Him show you how precious you are.

Enjoy Kay's continuing interview of Dorie N. Van Stone.

Then, as Kay suggests, go to the Gospel of John and begin to read it.

1. Mark every occurrence of the word *love* with a heart.

2. Every occurrence of the word *life.*

List what you learn. You'll find out how to have life and how to know the love of God that will hold you and transform you and keep you and will never leave you or forsake you.

You are precious to God! Let Him show you how precious you are!!

Healing After Sexual Abuse

PROGRAM **23**

TODAY

Kay's guest today is Dorie N. Van Stone (3rd of 3 programs).

INTRODUCTION

Whatever you're past, know this: that God knows you, that God loves you, that God wants to heal you. He wants to heal your marriage relationship. He wants to heal your sexual relationship. He wants you to know the love and security that He designed for the marriage bed. But that will only come as you get into the Word of God. And it was given to you that you might know truth and that truth might set you free. Jesus Christ, who is the way to God, who is truth, who offers you life, is the One that came that you might have life and have it abundantly.

Enjoy Kay's concluding interview of Dorie N. Van Stone.

If you haven't finished, continue marking *love* and *life* in the Gospel of John and listing what you learn.

Finally, list some thoughts from the following verses about the connection between forgiveness, cleansing from sin, and healing:

2 Chronicles 7:14

Jeremiah 30:16-20

Jeremiah 33:6-22.

PROGRAM 24

TODAY'S TEXTS

2 Corinthians 5:19

Proverbs 19:11; 13:10

Ephesians 4:26

James 1:19-20

Matthew 7:12

Proverbs 18:14

Ephesians 4:29

Job 16:4, 5

Proverbs 17:9

John 13:35

Proverbs 17:27; 13:15; 14:29-30

"Nevers" in Communication

INTRODUCTION

If a person is coming against you, if they're letting you have it, listen don't whip out the sword of your tongue and just lash at them and cut them back down. Never counterattack. You're going to be more the man. You're going to be more the woman if you just let them pull it out and you don't counterattack. If you just stop, if you listen. Watch their body language. Remember, a lot of communication is listening.

QUESTIONS

THE "NEVERS"
(Read all the listed verses)

1. **Never** say "never" or "always" with respect to bad attitudes or actions: "You'll *never* change; you'll *always* be the same."

    a. 1 Corinthians 5:19.

    1) How does Paul qualify (define) "reconciliation" here?

    2) If we extend this attitude and action toward people, how will it help communication with them?

    b. Proverbs 19:11.

    1) What is one aspect of man's glory?

    2) How can this help communication?

2. **Never** accuse a person of a feeling or attitude.

    a. Proverbs 13:10. What's a major cause of strife? How do we do it? How does it wreck good communication?

3. **Never** disallow someone's feelings.

    a. Ephesians 4:26. Can we stop negative emotions like anger from flaring up? Can we regulate them?

    b. James 1:19-20. What does James commend? Does the Word imply here that we can regulate emotions? What does anger *not* produce?

4. **Never** attack character.
   a. Matthew 7:12. What general approach to people does Jesus commend?

   b. Proverbs 18:14. What difference does a strong self-image (spirit) make? What does a broken spirit do? How does each promote or impair good communication?

   c. Ephesians 4:29. What words should we restrain? What words should we speak? How will these habits help?

   d. Job 16:15. What two powers does Job assign to words here?

5. **Never** counterattack.
   a. Proverbs 17:9. What love-action is described here? How does it aid good communication?

   b. John 13:35. What does Christian love for brethren prove?

6. **Never** discuss in anger.
   a. Proverbs 17:27. Write out the two qualities of a good communicator.

7. **Never** stop or discontinue a discussion.
   a. Proverbs 13:15. Describe the two pre-communication attitudes here and explain how they help or hinder good communication.

   b. Proverbs 14:29-30. Write down the good and bad emotions that help or hinder good communication.

Prayer

Father, so much great wisdom and counsel from Your Word, so much to think about, so much to plan and do! You've overwhelmingly impressed upon me the need to "get a grip" on my attitudes, thoughts, and emotions before I attempt to communicate. Help me control what I can and cause Your Spirit to overpower and restrain the rest. Give me a heart of reconciliation, a heart that pre-forgives people, that does not impute their trespasses when they occur. Guard my heart from jealousy, envy, and pride that cause strife. Make me pre-think how I want to be treated before I treat anyone in any given situation. I ask for these godly qualities so that all my communication will heal and encourage people. In Jesus' name I pray, Amen!

Today's Texts

2 Corinthians 5:19

19 namely, that God was in Christ reconciling the world to Himself, not counting their trespasses against them, and He has committed to us the word of reconciliation.

Proverbs 19:11

11 A man's discretion makes him slow to anger, and it is his glory to overlook a transgression.

Proverbs 13:10

10 Through insolence comes nothing but strife, But wisdom is with those who receive counsel.

Ephesians 4:26

26 BE ANGRY, AND *yet* DO NOT SIN; do not let the sun go down on your anger,

James 1:19-20

19 This you know, my beloved brethren. But everyone must be quick to hear, slow to speak *and* slow to anger;

20 for the anger of man does not achieve the righteousness of God.

Matthew 7:12

12 "In everything, therefore, treat people the same way you want them to treat you, for this is the Law and the Prophets."

Proverbs 18:14

14 The spirit of a man can endure his sickness, but *as for* a broken spirit who can bear it?

Ephesians 4:29

29 Let no unwholesome word proceed from your mouth, but only such *a word* as is good for edification according to the need *of the moment,* so that it will give grace to those who hear.

Job 16:4, 5

4 "I too could speak like you, if I were in your place. I could compose words against you and shake my head at you.

5 "I could strengthen you with my mouth, and the solace of my lips could lessen *your pain.*"

Proverbs 17:9

9 He who conceals a transgression seeks love, but he who repeats a matter separates intimate friends.

John 13:35

35 "By this all men will know that you are My disciples, if you have love for one another."

Proverbs 17:27

17 He who restrains his words has knowledge, and he who has a cool spirit is a man of understanding.

Proverbs 13:15

15 Good understanding produces favor, but the way of the treacherous is hard.

Proverbs 14:29-30

29 He who is slow to anger has great understanding, but he who is quick-tempered exalts folly.

30 A tranquil heart is life to the body, but passion is rottenness to the bones.

What God Says About Sex In Marriage

PROGRAM 25

TODAY'S TEXTS
Genesis 2:22-24
1 Corinthians 6:13-16
Genesis 1:28
Proverbs 5:15-19
1 Corinthians 7:1-5, 26-27

CROSS-REFERENCES
Hebrews 13:4

INTRODUCTION

Sex in marriage is not something that is just to be a function. Sex in marriage is not just intended for procreation. Sex in marriage is intended for pleasure. But that pleasure has to come God's way. You say, "I don't even want to have sex with him!" Well, we're going to talk about that later and we're going to talk about why you don't want to have sex. But let me just say this, because I want you to see that sex is ordained by God. And that God sees it as something beautiful. That's where we need to begin.

QUESTIONS

1. Review Genesis 2:22-24 and compare with 1 Corinthians 6:13-17.

   a. If a man plans on living with a woman, what should he do according to Genesis 2:24? List the actions and explain what each entails specifically.

   b. Explain the contrast between the temporal and eternal in 1 Corinthians 6:13. What did God create the body "for"? What does this imply about our priorities for *any* bodily action?

   c. What are we "members" of? If a man "joins himself to a prostitute is he "married" to her in God's eyes?

2. Now read Genesis 1:28 and Proverbs 5:15-18.

   a. What is the *primary* purpose for sex?

   b. List the phrases in the Proverbs passage that emphasize the exclusivity of the sexual relation in marriage.

   c. Do any of the commands imply that one of God's intentions for sex is pleasure?

3. Read 1 Corinthians 7:1-5, 26-27.

    a. Do we know what "the things about which you [Corinthians] wrote" (1) are? Does v. 2 give any hint?

    b. What is one reason for a man to have a wife?

    c. Do husbands and wives have sexual *duties* to each other? How does "duty" relate to "pleasure"? Are husbands and wives bound to pleasure their spouses even if the act doesn't please them?

    d. What is the exception to this? Why is it important to resume normal relations afterward?

    e. What's the connection between vv. 26-27? What do you think "the present distress" (26) was that impinged on the wisdom of people remaining as they are when they're called into the kingdom (26, 27)?

Prayer

Father, I see the significance and gravity of "one flesh," particularly in the fact that a man who joins himself to a prostitute becomes "one flesh" with her. Guard me from becoming one flesh with anyone other than the person You have chosen for me for life. Guard me also from becoming "one spirit" in reality or fantasy with anyone other than the "one spirit" with You and Your people in Your Church (1 Corinthians 6:17). Lord, if You have destined me to marriage—rather than called me to singleness, like Jesus and Paul, for the kingdom of God's sake—enable me to raise up godly seed for Your purposes and derive all my pleasure from and only from my spouse. In Jesus' name, Amen!

Today's Texts

Genesis 2:22-24

22 The LORD God fashioned into a woman the rib which He had taken from the man, and brought her to the man.

23 The man said, "This is now bone of my bones, and flesh of my flesh; she shall be called Woman, because she was taken out of Man."

24 For this reason a man shall leave his father and his mother, and be joined to his wife; and they shall become one flesh.

1 Corinthians 6:13-17

13 Food is for the stomach and the stomach is for food, but God will do away with both of them. Yet the body is not for immorality, but for the Lord, and the Lord is for the body.

14 Now God has not only raised the Lord, but will also raise us up through His power.

15 Do you not know that your bodies are members of Christ? Shall I then take away the members of Christ and make them members of a prostitute? May it never be!

16 Or do you not know that the one who joins himself to a prostitute is one body with her? For He says, "THE TWO SHALL BECOME ONE FLESH."

17 But the one who joins himself to the Lord is one spirit *with Him.*

Genesis 1:28

28 God blessed them; and God said to them, "Be fruitful and multiply, and fill the earth, and subdue it; and rule over the fish of the sea and over the birds of the sky and over every living thing that moves on the earth."

Proverbs 5:15-19

15 Drink water from your own cistern and fresh water from your own well.

16 Should your springs be dispersed abroad, streams of water in the streets?

17 Let them be yours alone and not for strangers with you.

18 Let your fountain be blessed, and rejoice in the wife of your youth.

19 As a loving hind and a graceful doe, Let her breasts satisfy you at all times; Be exhilarated always with her love.

1 Corinthians 7:1-5, 26-27

1 Now concerning the things about which you wrote, it is good for a man not to touch a woman.

2 But because of immoralities, each man is to have his own wife, and each woman is to have her own husband.

3 The husband must fulfill his duty to his wife, and likewise also the wife to her husband.

4 The wife does not have authority over her own body, but the husband does; and likewise also the husband does not have authority over his own body, but the wife does.

5 Stop depriving one another, except by agreement for a time, so that you may devote yourselves to prayer, and come together again so that Satan will not tempt you because of your lack of self-control.

26 I think then that this is good in view of the present distress, that it is good for a man to remain as he is.

27 Are you bound to a wife? Do not seek to be released. Are you released from a wife? Do not seek a wife.

Hebrews 13:4

4 Marriage is *to be held* in honor among all, and the *marriage* bed *is to be* undefiled; for fornicators and adulterers God will judge.

PROGRAM 26

TODAY'S TEXTS

Job 31:1
1 Corinthians 6:12—7:9

How to Have Good Sex in Marriage

INTRODUCTION

A lot of those women in the workplace are "on the make." And so if he's getting praise at work and admiration and she's smelling good and looking good and leaning close to him, know this, that usually a man wants to go home to his wife. And he wants to go home to his wife because that's where he's secure. That's not where he has to prove himself, where he has to be this king of sex. This is where he finds intimacy, the intimacy that god intended in sex.

QUESTIONS

1. Read Job 31:1.

   a. What does this verse have to say to someone who argues that marriage is "just" a piece of paper, or a wedding, or living together?

   b. What is it, truly?

   c. Who is it directed to—the Lord, the spouse, witnesses?

2. Now review 1 Corinthians 6:12—7:9 shading every reference to **body** in yellow.

   a. Again, what did God design our bodies "for" according to 6:13?

   b. Does Paul make a point about bodily pleasure *generally* in the first part of the verse? If so, could we read sexual (as opposed to hunger) categories into it? What's Paul's major point in *the context*?

   c. Which is more significant—physical/sexual memberships (one flesh) or membership in Christ (one spirit) according to 15-17?

   d. Is sex drive something Paul concedes (v.6) to in 7:1-2 and 7-9? What does he prefer?

Prayer

Father, since my "body is for the Lord," not "for" temporal physical pleasures like food which, with my stomach and every other physical organ, will be destroyed, I realize my first and eternal covenant with my eyes is to look to You. Keep me pure and holy in this regard, from gazing lustfully at a virgin whether I'm married or not and more generally from lusting for any other created object since this world "and its lusts" are passing away (1 John 2:17). Keep my mind, the eyes of my understanding, steadily on things above. Since my body is the temple of Your Holy Spirit, cause me to use its every appendage to benefit the members of Christ I am "joined" to—"one spirit" in You according to Your Word. And cause me to be physically content with the wife You have given me. In Jesus' name and for His sake and Your glory I pray for these things, Amen!

Today's Texts

Job 31:1

1 "I have made a covenant with my eyes; how then could I gaze at a virgin?"

1 Corinthians 6:12—7:9

12 All things are lawful for me, but not all things are profitable. All things are lawful for me, but I will not be mastered by anything.

13 Food is for the stomach and the stomach is for food, but God will do away with both of them. Yet the body is not for immorality, but for the Lord, and the Lord is for the body.

14 Now God has not only raised the Lord, but will also raise us up through His power.

15 Do you not know that your bodies are members of Christ? Shall I then take away the members of Christ and make them members of a prostitute? May it never be!

16 Or do you not know that the one who joins himself to a prostitute is one body *with her?* For He says, "THE TWO SHALL BECOME ONE FLESH."

17 But the one who joins himself to the Lord is one spirit *with Him.*

18 Flee immorality. Every other sin that a man commits is outside the body, but the immoral man sins against his own body.

19 Or do you not know that your body is a temple of the Holy Spirit who is in you, whom you have from God, and that you are not your own?

20 For you have been bought with a price: therefore glorify God in your body.

1 Now concerning the things about which you wrote, it is good for a man not to touch a woman.

2 But because of immoralities, each man is to have his own wife, and each woman is to have her own husband.

3 The husband must fulfill his duty to his wife, and likewise also the wife to her husband.

4 The wife does not have authority over her own body, but the husband *does;* and likewise also the husband does not have authority over his own body, but the wife *does.*

5 Stop depriving one another, except by agreement for a time, so that you may devote yourselves to prayer, and come together again so that Satan will not tempt you because of your lack of self-control.

6 But this I say by way of concession, not of command.

7 Yet I wish that all men were even as I myself am. However, each man has his own gift from God, one in this manner, and another in that.

8 But I say to the unmarried and to widows that it is good for them if they remain even as I.

9 But if they do not have self-control, let them marry; for it is better to marry than to burn with passion.

PROGRAM 27

TODAY'S TEXTS

Leviticus 20:7-8, 10-21; 18:6-25

What God Says About Sex Outside of Marriage

INTRODUCTION

Listen to me carefully, God's judgment is coming. The Judge is about to get up and He's about to come to earth to judge this world in righteousness and you and I need to be prepared. And you're prepared by listening to God and by believing what He says, by repenting. Repenting means a change of mind. And when I change my mind, it changes my direction.

QUESTIONS

1. Read Leviticus 20:7-8, 10-21, and 18:6-25.

   a. Contrasted with the nations that did whatever they wanted, what did God call Israel to do with respect to His statutes according to 20:7-8?

   b. In the verses that follow underline every sexual sin in red. Double underline the penalty.

Prayer

Father, I want to consecrate myself to you and be holy, unlike "the nations" you drove out of Canaan because of their defilements (18:24-25). Thank You for giving us so many details about sexual relations—which ones are holy and which ones are "abominations" in Your sight, not just far removed from but also counter to Your design and purposes. Lord, cause me to stand strong against every perversion of these holy laws in my culture. We commit our lives, our churches, and our countries to Your lead and safe keeping. Purge from us idolatry and sexual impurity, Lord; burn out this dross and purify us like silver so our children and children's children will call on Your name and be saved. In Jesus' name, Amen!

Today's Texts

Leviticus 20:7-8, 10-21

7 'You shall consecrate yourselves therefore and be holy, for I am the LORD your God.

8 'You shall keep My statutes and practice them; I am the LORD who sanctifies you.'

10 'If *there is* a man who commits adultery with another man's wife, one who commits adultery with his friend's wife, the adulterer and the adulteress shall surely be put to death.

11 'If *there is* a man who lies with his father's wife, he has uncovered his father's nakedness; both of them shall surely be put to death, their bloodguiltiness is upon them.

12 'If *there is* a man who lies with his daughter-in-law, both of them shall surely be put to death; they have committed incest, their bloodguiltiness is upon them.

13 'If *there is* a man who lies with a male as those who lie with a woman, both of them have committed a detestable act; they shall surely be put to death. Their bloodguiltiness is upon them.

14 'If *there is* a man who marries a woman and her mother, it is immorality; both he and they shall be burned with fire, so that there will be no immorality in your midst.

15 'If *there is* a man who lies with an animal, he shall surely be put to death; you shall also kill the animal.

16 'If *there is* a woman who approaches any animal to mate with it, you shall kill the woman and the animal; they shall surely be put to death. Their bloodguiltiness is upon them.

17 'If *there is* a man who takes his sister, his father's daughter or his mother's daughter, so that he sees her nakedness and she sees his nakedness, it is a disgrace; and they shall be cut off in the sight of the sons of their people. He has uncovered his sister's nakedness; he bears his guilt.

18 'If *there is* a man who lies with a menstruous woman and uncovers her nakedness, he has laid bare her flow, and she has exposed the flow of her blood; thus both of them shall be cut off from among their people.

19 'You shall also not uncover the nakedness of your mother's sister or of your father's sister, for such a one has made naked his blood relative; they will bear their guilt.

20 'If *there is* a man who lies with his uncle's wife he has uncovered his uncle's nakedness; they will bear their sin. They will die childless.

21 'If *there is* a man who takes his brother's wife, it is abhorrent; he has uncovered his brother's nakedness. They will be childless.'

Leviticus 18:6-25

6 'None of you shall approach any blood relative of his to uncover nakedness; I am the LORD.

7 'You shall not uncover the nakedness of your father, that is, the nakedness of your mother. She is your mother; you are not to uncover her nakedness.

8 'You shall not uncover the nakedness of your father's wife; it is your father's nakedness.

9 'The nakedness of your sister, either your father's daughter or your mother's daughter, whether born at home or born outside, their nakedness you shall not uncover.

10 'The nakedness of your son's daughter or your daughter's daughter, their nakedness you shall not uncover; for their nakedness is yours.

11 'The nakedness of your father's wife's daughter, born to your father, she is your sister, you shall not uncover her nakedness.

12 'You shall not uncover the nakedness of your father's sister; she is your father's blood relative.

13 'You shall not uncover the nakedness of your mother's sister, for she is your mother's blood relative.

14 'You shall not uncover the nakedness of your father's brother; you shall not approach his wife, she is your aunt.

15 'You shall not uncover the nakedness of your daughter-in-law; she is your son's wife, you shall not uncover her nakedness.

16 'You shall not uncover the nakedness of your brother's wife; it is your brother's nakedness.

17 'You shall not uncover the nakedness of a woman and of her daughter, nor shall you take her son's daughter or her daughter's daughter, to uncover her nakedness; they are blood relatives. It is lewdness.

18 'You shall not marry a woman in addition to her sister as a rival while she is alive, to uncover her nakedness.

19 'Also you shall not approach a woman to uncover her nakedness during her menstrual impurity.

20 'You shall not have intercourse with your neighbor's wife, to be defiled with her.

21 'You shall not give any of your offspring to offer them to Molech, nor shall you profane the name of your God; I am the LORD.

22 'You shall not lie with a male as one lies with a female; it is an abomination.

23 'Also you shall not have intercourse with any animal to be defiled with it, nor shall any woman stand before an animal to mate with it; it is a perversion.

24 'Do not defile yourselves by any of these things; for by all these the nations which I am casting out before you have become defiled.

25 'For the land has become defiled, therefore I have brought its punishment upon it, so the land has spewed out its inhabitants.'

Consequences of Immorality

PROGRAM 28

TODAY'S TEXTS
Romans 1:21-27
Proverbs 6:23-35; 7:6-27

CROSS-REFERENCES
1 Corinthians 6:18; 6:9-10

INTRODUCTION

Have you ever visited a harlot? Have you ever gone to a house of prostitution? Have you ever driven down certain streets because you know who's going to be standing on those street corners and you know that you can get what you want in any shape, in any form, in any size, any sort of perversion? All you have to do is pay for it. You are lacking sense if you head that way. And you are going to destroy yourself.

QUESTIONS

1. Read Romans 1:21-23. List the things that happen to the minds and hearts of those who do not honor God or give him thanks.

2. Now read vv. 24-25.
   a. What does God do to these people?

   b. What are their lusts redirected toward?

   c. Without writing down graphic details, how do they "dishonor their bodies"?

   d. How do they change epistemologically—that is, what do they turn *from* and *to* for their *source of knowledge?* Can you give some examples of this today?

   e. How about their object of faith, worship, and service—what do they turn *from* and *to?* Again, can you give some modern examples?

3. What's next in the chain of depravity according to vv. 26-27?

   a. What do the women do?

   b. What do the men do?

   c. Again skipping details, what kinds of acts are in mind?

   d. Most importantly, how are these acts *physically, emotionally* and *spiritually* harmful?

     1) Physically?

     2) Emotionally?

     3) Spiritually?

4. Review Proverbs 6:23-35 and 7:6-27.

   a. What risk do the adulterer and adulteress take?

   b. How does this danger compare with the bad consequences in Romans 1?

5. Now read **Cross-references** 1 Corinthians 6:18 and 6:9-10.

   a. What's unique about sexual sins according to v. 18? What are the implications?

   b. Besides adulterers and adulteresses "getting caught" (Proverbs above) and suffering moral degradation (Romans above) are there *eternal* consequences for sexual sins?

Prayer

Father, I can see where man has come from and where he has gone thanks to Your Word in Romans 1. At the beginning we knew You, honored You, and gave You thanks. Then we fell into futile speculation and darkness, exchanging the glory of your eternal attributes for corruptible forms and Your truth for lies. We defied and defiled Your holy covenant of marriage and substituted for it every form of temporary, superficial and self-serving commitment. From there we degraded to unnatural lusts and indecent acts that hurt us every conceivable way. Knowing that these things have horrible temporal and eternal consequences for us individually and corporately, we ask you to turn ungodliness away from our families, churches, schools, industries, government and country. Turn us back to you, Lord; revive our hearts so that we call upon You and obey Your statutes. In Jesus' name we pray, Amen!

Today's Texts

Romans 1:21-27

21 For even though they knew God, they did not honor Him as God or give thanks, but they became futile in their speculations, and their foolish heart was darkened.

22 Professing to be wise, they became fools,

23 and exchanged the glory of the incorruptible God for an image in the form of corruptible man and of birds and four-footed animals and crawling creatures.

24 Therefore God gave them over in the lusts of their hearts to impurity, so that their bodies would be dishonored among them.

25 For they exchanged the truth of God for a lie, and worshiped and served the creature rather than the Creator, who is blessed forever. Amen.

26 For this reason God gave them over to degrading passions; for their women exchanged the natural function for that which is unnatural,

27 and in the same way also the men abandoned the natural function of the woman and burned in their desire toward one another, men with men committing indecent acts and receiving in their own persons the due penalty of their error.

Proverbs 6:23-35

23 For the commandment is a lamp and the teaching is light; and reproofs for discipline are the way of life

24 To keep you from the evil woman, from the smooth tongue of the adulteress.

25 Do not desire her beauty in your heart, nor let her capture you with her eyelids.

26 For on account of a harlot *one is reduced* to a loaf of bread, and an adulteress hunts for the precious life.

27 Can a man take fire in his bosom and his clothes not be burned?

28 Or can a man walk on hot coals and his feet not be scorched?

29 So is the one who goes in to his neighbor's wife; whoever touches her will not go unpunished.

30 Men do not despise a thief if he steals to satisfy himself when he is hungry;

31 But when he is found, he must repay sevenfold; he must give all the substance of his house.

32 The one who commits adultery with a woman is lacking sense; he who would destroy himself does it.

33 Wounds and disgrace he will find, and his reproach will not be blotted out.

34 For jealousy enrages a man, And he will not spare in the day of vengeance.

35 He will not accept any ransom, nor will he be satisfied though you give many gifts.

Proverbs 7:6-27

6 For at the window of my house I looked out through my lattice,

7 And I saw among the naive, and discerned among the youths a young man lacking sense,

8 Passing through the street near her corner; and he takes the way to her house,

9 In the twilight, in the evening, in the middle of the night and *in* the darkness.

10 And behold, a woman *comes* to meet him, dressed as a harlot and cunning of heart.

11 *She is* boisterous and rebellious, her feet do not remain at home;

12 She is now in the streets, now in the squares, and lurks by every corner.

13 So she seizes him and kisses him and with a brazen face she says to him:

14 "I was due to offer peace offerings; today I have paid my vows.

15 "Therefore I have come out to meet you, to seek your presence earnestly, and I have found you.

16 "I have spread my couch with coverings, with colored linens of Egypt.

17 "I have sprinkled my bed with myrrh, aloes and cinnamon.

18 "Come, let us drink our fill of love until morning; let us delight ourselves with caresses.

19 "For my husband is not at home, he has gone on a long journey;

20 He has taken a bag of money with him, at the full moon he will come home."

21 With her many persuasions she entices him; with her flattering lips she seduces him.

22 Suddenly he follows her as an ox goes to the slaughter, Or as *one in* fetters to the discipline of a fool,

23 Until an arrow pierces through his liver; as a bird hastens to the snare, so he does not know that it will cost him his life.

24 Now therefore, *my* sons, listen to me, and pay attention to the words of my mouth.

25 Do not let your heart turn aside to her ways, do not stray into her paths.

26 For many are the victims she has cast down, and numerous are all her slain.

27 Her house is the way to Sheol, descending to the chambers of death.

1 Corinthians 6:18, 9-10

18 Flee immorality. Every *other* sin that a man commits is outside the body, but the immoral man sins against his own body.

9 Or do you not know that the unrighteous will not inherit the kingdom of God? Do not be deceived; neither fornicators, nor idolaters, nor adulterers, nor effeminate, nor homosexuals,

10 nor thieves, nor *the* covetous, nor drunkards, nor revilers, nor swindlers, will inherit the kingdom of God.

How Do You Handle Temptation?

PROGRAM 29

TODAY'S TEXTS
2 Samuel 11:1-27

Job 31:9-12

Matthew 5:27

CROSS-REFERENCES
1 Corinthians 6:18

INTRODUCTION

Precious One, you need to learn how to handle temptation. Because when lust conceives, it brings forth sin. And sin brings forth a child and that child's name is death. You don't want to die. You want to live. And Jesus can set you free. Just listen to Him.

QUESTIONS

1. Read 2 Samuel 11:1-27.

   a. How many times should David have "stopped" in his progression toward adultery and follow-up sins?

   b. Where would you say he "tempted his own flesh"? Is this a good idea?

   c. What mental and physical sins was David guilty of *apart from* adultery?

   d. Do you think he felt guilty at any point? How do you think he handled it?

   e. Does sin often require more sin? What for? Is sin ever successful in the long run? Why not? Who plays the final card?

2. Now read Job 31:9-12.

   a. What does Job wish on himself if he has not been loyal to his wife?

   b. What kinds of punishment does the adulterer receive?

3. Finally read Matthew 5:27 and **Cross-Reference** 1 Corinthians 6:18.

   a. Is adultery only physical?

   b. What is Paul's counsel to the Corinthians?

   c. Would any of this have been good, wise counsel to David?

   d. How can these truths help us?

   e. How can we help others with them without sounding judgmental?

Prayer

Father, I realize from this terrifying episode in David's life how easy it is to slip from temptation to temptation thinking I can master my physical desires . . . until finally one overpowers me. And I realize how easy it is to rationalize guilt away and/or cover up. Lord, I know I can flee from some external objects that are pretty and/or alluring but fleeing from lusts that are natural to my flesh is extremely hard. Because the outside and the inside together are such a lethal combination, dangerous to my soul and even eternal destiny, I ask you to help me not just flee from lust but also to pursue righteousness with my whole heart, soul, mind, and body. I'm grateful that you provide a "way of escape" from every temptation common to man so I can endure it (1 Corinthians 10:13). I'll look for these "ways out" in the future; please help me recognize them. And if I fail, help me to confess and abandon my sin quickly! In Jesus' name I pray, Amen!

Today's Texts

2 Samuel 11:1-27

1 Then it happened in the spring, at the time when kings go out to battle, that David sent Joab and his servants with him and all Israel, and they destroyed the sons of Ammon and besieged Rabbah. But David stayed at Jerusalem.

2 Now when evening came David arose from his bed and walked around on the roof of the king's house, and from the roof he saw a woman bathing; and the woman was very beautiful in appearance.

3 So David sent and inquired about the woman. And one said, "Is this not Bathsheba, the daughter of Eliam, the wife of Uriah the Hittite?"

4 David sent messengers and took her, and when she came to him, he lay with her; and when she had purified herself from her uncleanness, she returned to her house.

5 The woman conceived; and she sent and told David, and said, "I am pregnant."

6 Then David sent to Joab, saying, "Send me Uriah the Hittite." So Joab sent Uriah to David.

7 When Uriah came to him, David asked concerning the welfare of Joab and the people and the state of the war.

8 Then David said to Uriah, "Go down to your house, and wash your feet." And Uriah went out of the king's house, and a present from the king was sent out after him.

9 But Uriah slept at the door of the king's house with all the servants of his lord, and did not go down to his house.

10 Now when they told David, saying, "Uriah did not go down to his house," David said to Uriah, "Have you not come from a journey? Why did you not go down to your house?"

11 Uriah said to David, "The ark and Israel and Judah are staying in temporary shelters, and my lord Joab and the servants of my lord are camping in the open field. Shall I then go to my house to eat and to drink and to lie with my wife? By your life and the life of your soul, I will not do this thing."

12 Then David said to Uriah, "Stay here today also, and tomorrow I will let you go." So Uriah remained in Jerusalem that day and the next.

13 Now David called him, and he ate and drank before him, and he made him drunk; and in the evening he went out to lie on his bed with his lord's servants, but he did not go down to his house.

14 Now in the morning David wrote a letter to Joab and sent it by the hand of Uriah.

15 He had written in the letter, saying, "Place Uriah in the front line of the fiercest battle and withdraw from him, so that he may be struck down and die."

16 So it was as Joab kept watch on the city, that he put Uriah at the place where he knew there were valiant men.

17 The men of the city went out and fought against Joab, and some of the people among David's servants fell; and Uriah the Hittite also died.

18 Then Joab sent and reported to David all the events of the war.

19 He charged the messenger, saying, "When you have finished telling all the events of the war to the king,

20 and if it happens that the king's wrath rises and he says to you, 'Why did you go so near to the city to fight? Did you not know that they would shoot from the wall?

21 'Who struck down Abimelech the son of Jerubbesheth? Did not a woman throw an upper millstone on him from the wall so that he died at Thebez? Why did you go so near the wall?'—then you shall say, 'Your servant Uriah the Hittite is dead also.' "

22 So the messenger departed and came and reported to David all that Joab had sent him to tell.

23 The messenger said to David, "The men prevailed against us and came out against us in the field, but we pressed them as far as the entrance of the gate.

24 "Moreover, the archers shot at your servants from the wall; so some of the king's servants are dead, and your servant Uriah the Hittite is also dead."

25 Then David said to the messenger, "Thus you shall say to Joab, 'Do not let this thing displease you, for the sword devours one as well as another; make your battle against the city stronger and overthrow it'; and so encourage him."

26 Now when the wife of Uriah heard that Uriah her husband was dead, she mourned for her husband.

27 When the time of mourning was over, David sent and brought her to his house and she became his wife; then she bore him a son. But the thing that David had done was evil in the sight of the LORD.

Job 31:9-12

9 "If my heart has been enticed by a woman, or I have lurked at my neighbor's doorway,

10 May my wife grind for another, and let others kneel down over her.

11 "For that would be a lustful crime; moreover, it would be an iniquity punishable by judges.

12 "For it would be fire that consumes to Abaddon, and would uproot all my increase."

Matthew 5:27

27 "You have heard that it was said, 'YOU SHALL NOT COMMIT ADULTERY';

28 but I say to you that everyone who looks at a woman with lust for her has already committed adultery with her in his heart."

1 Corinthians 6:18

18 Flee immorality. Every other sin that a man commits is outside the body, but the immoral man sins against his own body.

What Do You Do After You've Yielded to Temptation?

PROGRAM 30

TODAY'S TEXTS
2 Samuel 11 (Lesson 29)
1 John 1:9
Proverbs 28:13
2 Corinthians 7:8-10
James 4:1-2

INTRODUCTION

God is saying that He will forgive sins, that He is merciful, that He is full of loving-kindness, and that if we will do what He says, then God will meet us at our point of obedience. So 1 John 1:9 says *If we confess our sins, if we name our sin for what it is, He, God is faithful and just to forgive us our sin, and to cleanse us from all unrighteousness.*

QUESTIONS

1. Review Lesson 29—David's adultery with Bathsheba and murder of Uriah the Hittite—with respect to how he handled these sins as they accumulated.

2. Now read 1 John 1:9.
   a. What does "confess" mean? (See **Did You Know?**)

   b. What two things will God do when we confess our sins to Him?

      1) _____

      2) _____

   c. Did David do this right away? What prompted him? (Read 2 Samuel 12.)

3. Read Proverbs 28:13.
   a. What happens to those who conceal their sins?

   b. What happens to those who confess and forsake their sins?

   c. What did David do first and last and why?

4. Read 2 Corinthians 7:8-10.
   a. Why did Paul not regret causing the Corinthians sorrow?

DID YOU KNOW?

ὁμολογῶμεν (*homologo-men:* 1John 1:9) from *homo,* same, and *logeo,* to speak. To verbally agree with someone.

   b. What are the characteristics of "sorrow according to the will of God"?

   c. What are the characteristics of "sorrow of the world"?

5. Now read James 4:1-2.
   a. What causes quarrels and conflicts?

   b. What can unsatisfied lust lead to?

   c. Was that the case with David? What should he have done and when?

Prayer

Father, I see again how powerful lust is since unsatisfied it can produce even murder. I pray that You will fill me with the fruit of Your Spirit—love, joy, peace, patience, kindness, goodness, faithfulness, gentleness, and self-control—and empower me to repent from the fruit of my flesh—immorality, impurity, sensuality, idolatry, sorcery, enmities, strife, jealousy, outbursts of anger, disputes, dissensions, factions, envying, drunkenness and carousing. Since I am so short the perfections and so long the rest, thank You for Your promise to forgive and cleanse me when I confess sins. In Jesus' name, Amen!

Today's Texts

1 John 1:9
9 If we confess our sins, He is faithful and righteous to forgive us our sins and to cleanse us from all un-righteousness.

Proverbs 28:13
13 He who conceals his transgressions will not prosper, but he who confesses and forsakes them will find compassion.

2 Corinthians 7:8-10
8 For though I caused you sorrow by my letter, I do not regret it; though I did regret it—*for* I see that that letter caused you sorrow, though only for a while—

9 I now rejoice, not that you were made sorrowful, but that you were made sorrowful *to the point of* repentance; for you were made sorrowful according to *the will of* God, so that you might not suffer loss in anything through us.

10 For the sorrow that is according to *the will of* God produces a repentance without regret, *leading* to salvation, but the sorrow of the world produces death.

James 4:1-2
1 What is the source of quarrels and conflicts among you? Is not the source your pleasures that wage war in your members?

2 You lust and do not have; *so* you commit murder. You are envious and cannot obtain; *so* you fight and quarrel. You do not have because you do not ask.

Temptation– Consider the Cost

PROGRAM 31

TODAY'S TEXTS
2 Samuel 11 (Lesson 29)
Numbers 32:23
Lamentations 1:8-9
Proverbs 28:13
1 Corinthians 10:13
2 Thessalonians 1:6-10
2 Samuel 12:1-14
Leviticus 6:1-7

INTRODUCTION

When you receive Jesus Christ, you pass from death to life. You're going to live forever and ever in the presence of God. And someday, God's going to remove all sin and He is going to wipe away every tear. And there's not going to be any more tears and no more sorrow and no more death and all the former things of your life will pass away. They won't bother you anymore. They won't haunt you anymore. They won't torment you anymore.

QUESTIONS

1. Review Lesson 29 again.

2. For each of the following verses, write out the consequence(s) of sin:
   a. Numbers 32:23.

   b. Lamentations 1:8-9

   c. Proverbs 28:13

3. Now write out God's promises to us when we're obedient:
   a. 1 Corinthians 10:13

   b. 2 Thessalonians 1:6-10

4. Now let's see what happened to David. Read 2 Samuel 12:1-14.
   a. Explain the parable Nathan told David by identifying:
   1) The rich man

   2) The poor man

   3) The ewe

   b. Why did David get so angry when he heard this story?

   c. What did he demand for "restitution"?

   d. What did Nathan accuse David of? Besides Uriah and Bathsheba who else were damaged by David's sins?

   e. What three terrible judgments does Nathan pronounce on David? While David attempted to sin in secret, was God going to judge him in secret?

     1)

     2)

     3)

   f. How did David respond to this pronouncement? Did these judgments impact Israel as a nation in the long run? If so, how?

   g. What did Nathan say after David responded? What did he mean when he said "you shall not die" (v. 13)? What is this connected to immediately prior? What kind of "death" do you think Nathan had in mind?

5. How do your answers to questions 2. and 3. apply to David in terms of what he should and should not have done and in terms of what we need to do?

6. Read Leviticus 6:1-7. What must a man who robs, extorts, or borrows a deposit do in order to *restore* himself?

   a. v. 5:

   b. vv. 6-7:

Prayer

Father, it's easy for me to criticize others, even a great king like David, "a man after Your own heart." After all you delivered into his hands, he presumptuously sinned against You terribly—committing adultery, murdering, giving Your enemies occasion to sin. And Your judgments were terrible, culminating in the split of Your nation only two generations later. Lord, even though you provide external ways of escape, I need the power of Your Spirit to "strive against" my internal flesh, to overpower and eventually kill it. This is my deeper enemy and my deeper salvation. Work in me to will and do Your good pleasure. Help me overcome the world, the god of this world, and my own raging lusts. Guard my integrity so I can guard Yours by not giving Your enemies occasions to blaspheme. Lead me in paths of righteousness for Your name's sake. I ask for these things in the name of the Son Your soul delights in, the Lord our righteousness, Amen!

Today's Texts

Numbers 32:23

23 "But if you will not do so, behold, you have sinned against the LORD, and be sure your sin will find you out."

Lamentations 1:8-9

8 Jerusalem sinned greatly, Therefore she has become an unclean thing. All who honored her despise her because they have seen her nakedness; even she herself groans and turns away.

9 Her uncleanness was in her skirts; she did not consider her future. Therefore she has fallen astonishingly; she has no comforter. "See, O LORD, my affliction, for the enemy has magnified himself!"

Proverbs 28:13

13 He who conceals his transgressions will not prosper, but he who confesses and forsakes them will find compassion.

1 Corinthians 10:13

13 No temptation has overtaken you but such as is common to man; and God is faithful, who will not allow you to be tempted beyond what you are able, but with the temptation will provide the way of escape also, so that you will be able to endure it.

2 Thessalonians 1:6-10

6 For after all it is *only* just for God to repay with affliction those who afflict you,

7 and *to give* relief to you who are afflicted and to us as well when the Lord Jesus will be revealed from heaven with His mighty angels in flaming fire,

8 dealing out retribution to those who do not know God and to those who do not obey the gospel of our Lord Jesus.

9 These will pay the penalty of eternal destruction, away from the presence of the Lord and from the glory of His power,

10 when He comes to be glorified in His saints on that day, and to be marveled at among all who have believed—for our testimony to you was believed.

2 Samuel 12:1-14

1 Then the LORD sent Nathan to David. And he came to him and said, "There were two men in one city, the one rich and the other poor.

2 "The rich man had a great many flocks and herds.

3 "But the poor man had nothing except one little ewe lamb which he bought and nourished; and it grew up together with him and his children. It would eat of his bread and drink of his cup and lie in his bosom, and was like a daughter to him.

4 "Now a traveler came to the rich man, and he was unwilling to take from his own flock or his own herd, To prepare for the wayfarer who had come to him; Rather he took the poor man's ewe lamb and prepared it for the man who had come to him."

5 Then David's anger burned greatly against the man, and he said to Nathan, "As the LORD lives, surely the man who has done this deserves to die.

6 "He must make restitution for the lamb fourfold, because he did this thing and had no compassion."

7 Nathan then said to David, "You are the man! Thus says the LORD God of Israel, 'It is I who anointed you king over Israel and it is I who delivered you from the hand of Saul.

8 'I also gave you your master's house and your master's wives into your care, and I gave you the house of Israel and Judah; and if that had been too little, I would have added to you many more things like these!

9 'Why have you despised the word of the LORD by doing evil in His sight? You have struck down Uriah the Hittite with the sword, have taken his wife to be your wife, and have killed him with the sword of the sons of Ammon.

10 'Now therefore, the sword shall never depart from your house, because you have despised Me and have taken the wife of Uriah the Hittite to be your wife.'

11 "Thus says the LORD, 'Behold, I will raise up evil against you from your own household; I will even take your wives before your eyes and give *them* to your companion, and he will lie with your wives in broad daylight.

12 'Indeed you did it secretly, but I will do this thing before all Israel, and under the sun.' "

13 Then David said to Nathan, "I have sinned against the LORD." And Nathan said to David, "The LORD also has taken away your sin; you shall not die.

14 "However, because by this deed you have given occasion to the enemies of the LORD to blaspheme, the child also that is born to you shall surely die."

Leviticus 6:1-7

1 Then the LORD spoke to Moses, saying,

2 "When a person sins and acts unfaithfully against the LORD, and deceives his companion in regard to a deposit or a security entrusted to him, or through robbery, or if he has extorted from his companion,

3 or has found what was lost and lied about it and sworn falsely, so that he sins in regard to any one of the things a man may do

4 then it shall be, when he sins and becomes guilty, that he shall restore what he took by robbery or what he got by extortion, or the deposit which was entrusted to him or the lost thing which he found,

5 or anything about which he swore falsely; he shall make restitution for it in full and add to it one-fifth more. He shall give it to the one to whom it belongs on the day he presents his guilt offering."

6 "Then he shall bring to the priest his guilt offering to the LORD, a ram without defect from the flock, according to your valuation, for a guilt offering,

7 and the priest shall make atonement for him before the LORD, and he will be forgiven for any one of the things which he may have done to incur guilt."

The Do's and Don'ts When You Are Tempted

PROGRAM **32**

TODAY'S TEXTS
2 Samuel 12:10, 11, 14
Psalm 73:1-20
James 1:13-15
Genesis 39:5-13

CROSS-REFERENCES
2 Samuel 12:8
Luke 11:4
Matthew 4:1

INTRODUCTION

You have the Word of the Lord. God is speaking to you. Not because I'm some prophet or anything. God is speaking to you because I'm reading you His Word, because we're going through it verse by verse. This is the Word of God. You've heard it. You've heard what God says about immorality. You've heard that your sins are going to find you out. You've heard what is evil. You've heard about a godly sorrow that leads to repentance and a worldly sorrow that leads to death. You've heard it. Now are you going to listen or are you not going to listen?

QUESTIONS

1. Review God's judgments on David in 2 Samuel 12:10, 11, 14.

   a. Did David's sin "find him out" (Numbers 32:23)? Can we sin "under-cover" against God? Can we ever "get away with it"?

   b. If you're familiar with Israel's subsequent history, how did God's "sword" in David's house work out shortly after Solomon's reign? What did David personally suffer?

2. Now read Psalm 73:1-20.

   a. Did Asaph have a moral problem with the present status of rich people?

   b. Write down what appear to be God's blessings in the short run.

   c. Where is the turning point in Asaph's thinking? Circle the verse(s).

   d. Briefly summarize his thoughts about the long-term future of the rich. Should the wealthy consider such thoughts? Why or why not?

   e. Do you think David's wealth and status contributed to his presumption—thinking he could "get away with just about anything"—in spite of the fact that God had given him all these things?

   f. Did God Himself make a point of this? (Review **Cross-reference** 2 Samuel 12:8.) Could David have taken his lusts, so to speak, to the Lord for relief?

3. Now read James 1:13-15.
   a. Is temptation sin? Is lust sin?

   b. Did God tempt David with Bathsheba? Did He "lead . . . into temptation"? (See Cross-references Luke 11:4; Matthew 4:1.)

   c. What source of David's temptation was he responsible for?

   d. What do lust and sin respectively produce?

4. Finally, read the account of Joseph and Potiphar's wife in Genesis 39:5-13.
   a. What had Pharaoh put Joseph in charge of?

   b. Why was Potiphar's wife attracted to Joseph?

   c. What did she do to entice Joseph?

   d. How did Joseph respond initially? What were his two moral arguments:
     1) With respect to his "master"?

     2) With respect to "God"?

   e. Did Potiphar's wife press on?

   f. Did this "end well" for Joseph?

   g. Is it always easy to take a stand for God's precepts against persevering evils? What occasions are the most difficult?

5. Briefly compare David's encounter with Bathsheba and Joseph's with Potiphar's wife.

Prayer

Father, I see how easily wealth and status take our eyes off you and put them on things of the world. You gave David everything and told him he could have asked You for more. Yet he mysteriously chose to glance away and do something without reference to You, without first asking for Your lead. How often my own thoughts drift like this. Lord, You promised perfect peace to those who keep their eyes on You. Keep my mind from drifting. I know wealth and status are short-term comforts but long-term deceits and that eternal prosperity comes only from You, from Your truth. Thank You for including David and Joseph's best and worst experiences in Your Word so that I would have Your fear and Your promise ever before me, even the promise of gracious restoration when I fail and sin like David. In Jesus' name, Amen!

Today's Texts

2 Samuel 12:10, 11, 14

10 'Now therefore, the sword shall never depart from your house, because you have despised Me and have taken the wife of Uriah the Hittite to be your wife.'

11 "Thus says the LORD, 'Behold, I will raise up evil against you from your own household; I will even take your wives before your eyes and give them to your companion, and he will lie with your wives in broad daylight.'"

14 "However, because by this deed you have given occasion to the enemies of the LORD to blaspheme, the child also that is born to you shall surely die."

Psalm 73:1-20

1 A Psalm of Asaph. Surely God is good to Israel, to those who are pure in heart!

2 But as for me, my feet came close to stumbling, my steps had almost slipped.

3 For I was envious of the arrogant as I saw the prosperity of the wicked.

4 For there are no pains in their death, and their body is fat.

5 They are not in trouble *as other* men, nor are they plagued like mankind.

6 Therefore pride is their necklace; the garment of violence covers them.

7 Their eye bulges from fatness; the imaginations of *their* heart run riot.

8 They mock and wickedly speak of oppression; they speak from on high.

9 They have set their mouth against the heavens, and their tongue parades through the earth.

10 Therefore his people return to this place, and waters of abundance are drunk by them.

11 They say, "How does God know? And is there knowledge with the Most High?"

12 Behold, these are the wicked; and always at ease, they have increased in wealth.

13 Surely in vain I have kept my heart pure and washed my hands in innocence;

14 For I have been stricken all day long and chastened every morning.

15 If I had said, "I will speak thus," Behold, I would have betrayed the generation of Your children.

16 When I pondered to understand this, it was troublesome in my sight

17 Until I came into the sanctuary of God; then I perceived their end.

18 Surely You set them in slippery places; you cast them down to destruction.

19 How they are destroyed in a moment! They are utterly swept away by sudden terrors!

20 Like a dream when one awakes, O Lord, when aroused, You will despise their form.

James 1:13-15

13 Let no one say when he is tempted, "I am being tempted by God"; for God cannot be tempted by evil, and He Himself does not tempt anyone.

14 But each one is tempted when he is carried away and enticed by his own lust.

15 Then when lust has conceived, it gives birth to sin; and when sin is accomplished, it brings forth death.

Genesis 39:5-13

5 It came about that from the time he made him overseer in his house and over all that he owned, the LORD blessed the Egyptian's house on account of Joseph; thus the LORD'S blessing was upon all that he owned, in the house and in the field.

6 So he left everything he owned in Joseph's charge; and with him *there* he did not concern himself with anything except the food which he ate. Now Joseph was handsome in form and appearance.

7 It came about after these events that his master's wife looked with desire at Joseph, and she said, "Lie with me."

8 But he refused and said to his master's wife, "Behold, with me *here*, my master does not concern himself with anything in the house, and he has put all that he owns in my charge.

9 "There is no one greater in this house than I, and he has withheld nothing from me except you, because you are his wife. How then could I do this great evil and sin against God?"

10 As she spoke to Joseph day after day, he did not listen to her to lie beside her or be with her.

11 Now it happened one day that he went into the house to do his work, and none of the men of the household was there inside.

12 She caught him by his garment, saying, "Lie with me!" And he left his garment in her hand and fled, and went outside.

13 When she saw that he had left his garment in her hand and had fled outside,

2 Samuel 12:8

8 'I also gave you your master's house and your master's wives into your care, and I gave you the house of Israel and Judah; and if *that had been* too little, I would have added to you many more things like these!'

Luke 11:4

4 'And forgive us our sins, for we ourselves also forgive everyone who is indebted to us. And lead us not into temptation.' "

Matthew 4:1

1 Then Jesus was led up by the Spirit into the wilderness to be tempted by the devil.

When You Commit Adultery

INTRODUCTION

I want you to understand that when you commit adultery, you are defrauding another person. You're defrauding the person that you're sleeping with. And you are defrauding, if they are married, you are defrauding someone's husband or someone's wife. And you've got to know that the Lord is "the avenger in all these things" (1 Thessalonians 4:6). In other words, you're going to have to deal with God.

TODAY'S TEXTS

Exodus 20:14

Malachi 2:10-15

Genesis 15:9-12, 17-18

Galatians 5:16, 22-24

1 Corinthians 6:18

1 Thessalonians 4:3-6

QUESTIONS

1. Read Exodus 20:14.

   a. Is adultery optional for the believer?

   b. Who's saying "No!" to it here?

   c. Does the rank of the authority make the crime serious?

2. What do you learn about holy marriage from God's covenants in
   a. Malachi 2:10-15?

   a. Genesis 15:9-12, 17-18?

3. Now read Galatians 5:16, 22-24.

   a. What ethical advantages does a believer have according to vv. 16 and 24?

b. List the nine qualities of the one fruit of the Spirit. Check off the ones you think especially help to offset and overcome sexual lust.

4. Review 1 Corinthians 6:18 and read 1 Thessalonians 4:3-6.

a. What is the believer to specifically "flee" and why?

b. What is the will of God for the believer

1) Generally?

2) Particularly?

c. What are all kinds of sexual immorality according to 1 Thessalonians 4:6?

d. Strictly according to the text, is God passively uninvolved or actively involved after people commit fornication and adultery? In what sense—what does He do? Have you ever seen this happen?

Prayer

Father, I am in covenant with you since I am Abraham's seed through faith in the Lord Jesus. Cause me to realize every day the solemnity and binding nature of this covenant, particularly Your will for my sanctification. Guard me from sexual lust and expression of every sort that defraud my neighbors. Help me possess my own vessel with the Spirit's fruit of self-control. Keep me in holy covenant with You and with Your people. In Jesus' name, Amen!

Today's Texts

Exodus 20:14

14 "You shall not commit adultery."

Malachi 2:10

10 "Do we not all have one father? Has not one God created us? Why do we deal treacherously each against his brother so as to profane the covenant of our fathers?"

Genesis 15:9-12, 17-18

9 So He said to him, "Bring Me a three year old heifer, and a three year old female goat, and a three year old ram, and a turtledove, and a young pigeon."

10 Then he brought all these to Him and cut them in two, and laid each half opposite the other; but he did not cut the birds.

11 The birds of prey came down upon the carcasses, and Abram drove them away.

12 Now when the sun was going down, a deep sleep fell upon Abram; and behold, terror *and* great darkness fell upon him.

17 It came about when the sun had set, that it was very dark, and behold, *there appeared* a smoking oven and a flaming torch which passed between these pieces.

18 On that day the LORD made a covenant with Abram, saying, "To your descendants I have given this land, From the river of Egypt as far as the great river, the river Euphrates:"

Galatians 5:16, 22-24

16 But I say, walk by the Spirit, and you will not carry out the desire of the flesh.

22 But the fruit of the Spirit is love, joy, peace, patience, kindness, goodness, faithfulness,

23 gentleness, self-control; against such things there is no law.

24 Now those who belong to Christ Jesus have crucified the flesh with its passions and desires.

1 Corinthians 6:18

18 Flee immorality. Every *other* sin that a man commits is outside the body, but the immoral man sins against his own body.

1 Thessalonians 4:3-6

3 For this is the will of God, your sanctification; *that is,* that you abstain from sexual immorality;

4 that each of you know how to possess his own vessel in sanctification and honor,

5 not in lustful passion, like the Gentiles who do not know God;

6 *and* that no man transgress and defraud his brother in the matter because the Lord is *the* avenger in all these things, just as we also told you before and solemnly warned *you.*

PROGRAM **34**

How To Approach God After You Have Sinned

TODAY'S TEXTS

Psalm 51:1-12

Leviticus 17:11

1 Peter 1:18-19

Hebrews 9:22; 10:29

1 John 1:7

Hebrews 11:6

Exodus 34:6

1 John 1:8-9

CROSS-REFERENCES

James 4:12

INTRODUCTION

You know the Bible says "Without faith, it's impossible to please God. Those who come to God must believe that He is . . . ." He's believing what God said about Himself: ". . . the Lord, the Lord God, compassionate and gracious, slow to anger, abounding in loving-kindness and truth." You see, if you're going to deal with adultery properly, you have to deal with it in truth.

QUESTIONS

1. Read Psalm 51:1-12.

   a. What attributes of God does David appeal to in v. 1 for God to blot out his sins?

   b. Can we easily shake our sins off (v. 3)?

   c. Who do we sin against ultimately (v. 4)? Why do you think? (See **Cross-reference** James 4:12 for a hint.)

   d. Where is the locus (center-point) of sin? What then does God have to do to save and cleanse us?

   e. List the *ways* David asks God to save him.

   f. According to David are believers ever hopelessly lost, beyond restoration?

2. What do the following verses tell us precisely about the connection of blood to our salvation?

   a. Leviticus 17:11

   b. 1 Peter 1:18-19

   c. Hebrews 9:22

   d. Hebrews 10:29

   e. 1 John 1:7

3. What do the following tell us about *whether* and *what* we must believe about God in order to please Him?

   a. Hebrews 11:6

   b. Exodus 34:6

4. How do we deal with sin after we've been born again according to 1 John 1:8-9?

Prayer

Father, I know I'm a sinner by nature and that I need Your truth and Spirit in my innermost being. I'm so grateful that You are gracious, that you blot out sins by Your compassion and loving-kindness. I thank You for the precious blood of Jesus that not only redeemed me but also cleanses me daily as I confess my sins. Thank You for securing my eternal life, promising that You will never cast out any who come to you in faith believing that You exist, that you reward those who come to You, and that You are compassionate and gracious, slow to anger, and abounding in loving-kindness and truth. In Jesus' name, Amen!

Today's Texts

Psalm 51:1-12

1 For the choir director. A Psalm of David, when Nathan the prophet came to him, after he had gone in to Bathsheba. Be gracious to me, O God, according to Your loving-kindness; according to the greatness of Your compassion blot out my transgressions.

2 Wash me thoroughly from my iniquity and cleanse me from my sin.

3 For I know my transgressions, and my sin is ever before me.

4 Against You, You only, I have sinned and done what is evil in Your sight, So that You are justified when You speak And blameless when You judge.

5 Behold, I was brought forth in iniquity, and in sin my mother conceived me.

6 Behold, You desire truth in the innermost being, and in the hidden part You will make me know wisdom.

7 Purify me with hyssop, and I shall be clean; Wash me, and I shall be whiter than snow.

8 Make me to hear joy and gladness, Let the bones which You have broken rejoice.

9 Hide Your face from my sins And blot out all my iniquities.

10 Create in me a clean heart, O God, and renew a steadfast spirit within me.

11 Do not cast me away from Your presence and do not take Your Holy Spirit from me.

12 Restore to me the joy of Your salvation And sustain me with a willing spirit.

Leviticus 17:11

11 'For the life of the flesh is in the blood, and I have given it to you on the altar to make atonement for your souls; for it is the blood by reason of the life that makes atonement.'

1 Peter 1:18-19

18 knowing that you were not redeemed with perishable things like silver or gold from your futile way of life inherited from your forefathers,

19 but with precious blood, as of a lamb unblemished and spotless, *the blood* of Christ.

Hebrews 9:22, 10:29

22 And according to the Law, *one may* almost say, all things are cleansed with blood, and without shedding of blood there is no forgiveness.

29 How much severer punishment do you think he will deserve who has trampled underfoot the Son of God, and has regarded as unclean the blood of the covenant by which he was sanctified, and has insulted the Spirit of grace?

1 John 1:7

7 but if we walk in the Light as He Himself is in the Light, we have fellowship with one another, and the blood of Jesus His Son cleanses us from all sin.

Hebrews 11:6

6 And without faith it is impossible to please *Him,* for he who comes to God must believe that He is and *that* He is a rewarder of those who seek Him.

Exodus 34:6

6 Then the LORD passed by in front of him and proclaimed, "The LORD, the LORD God, compassionate and gracious, slow to anger, and abounding in lovingkindness and truth;"

1 John 1:8-9

8 If we say that we have no sin, we are deceiving ourselves and the truth is not in us.

9 If we confess our sins, He is faithful and righteous to forgive us our sins and to cleanse us from all unrighteousness.

James 4:12

12 There is *only* one Lawgiver and Judge, the One who is able to save and to destroy; but who are you who judge your neighbor?

Wash Me, Cleanse Me O God

PROGRAM 35

INTRODUCTION

If you have sinned and you are truly a believer and you know that you're a believer because you've been changed and because His Spirit bears witness with your Spirit, then you simply come to Him and you confess that sin and you trust in Him and He will make you clean. He's the only one, Precious One, that can make you clean. So have you believed on Jesus Christ? Has your life ever changed?

TODAY'S TEXTS

Psalm 51:1-12

Leviticus 14:1-7

Isaiah 1:16-18

John 13:8-10; 10:10; 6:37

Hebrews 9:12; 10:10; 10:14

CROSS-REFERENCES

Hebrews 13:11-13

QUESTIONS

1. Review Psalm 51:1-12. Summarize the three segments using the titles Kay gave to each:

   a. vv. 1-2: _____

   b. vv. 3-6 _____

   c. vv. 7-14 _____

2. Now read Leviticus 14:1-7.

   a. What primary truth is God showing us in this ritual?

   b. When the act is performed, what happens to the leper?

   c. How does this ritual point to what Jesus Christ has done for us?

   d. What other ways can we approach God? Penance? Good works?

3. Now read Isaiah 1:16-18.

    a. What does God command His people to do generally?

    b. Does He give specific examples of what He wants them to do?

    c. Describe the "reasoning" the Lord wants His people to do with Him.

4. Read John 13:8-10.

    a. Why do you think Peter did not want Jesus to wash his feet? What's the *general* problem? Is this a problem for us today?

    b. How did Jesus respond to Peter? Was this a threat?

    c. Explain Jesus' contrast between bathing and washing feet.

    d. Had all the Twelve Apostles been bathed? Who do you suppose Jesus had in mind?

5. Write out key terms or phrases that highlight the believer's security in Christ from following verses:

    a. John 10:10

    b. John 6:37

    c. Hebrews 9:12

    d. Hebrews 10:10

    e. Hebrews 10:14

Prayer

Father, thank You for bathing me in the precious blood of Jesus. I'm so thankful I need to bathe in Him only once because of the eternal redemption He accomplished once for all time by His blood. But I'm also thankful that I can continue to come to Him to wash my feet daily. Thank You for Your Word, especially for the numerous types in the Old Testament that so clearly point to Christ and His work. The continuity between the two Testaments constantly amazes me and reminds me that You have always saved Your people the same way, through blood atonement and faith. Help me share this Word "outside the camp" as I bear Jesus' reproach in the world He Himself said would hate me because it first hated Him. I want to bring the light of Your Word to those who dwell in darkness. In Jesus' name I pray, Amen!

Today's Texts

Psalm 51:1-12

1 For the choir director. A Psalm of David, when Nathan the prophet came to him, after he had gone in to Bathsheba. Be gracious to me, O God, according to Your loving-kindness; according to the greatness of Your compassion blot out my transgressions.

2 Wash me thoroughly from my iniquity and cleanse me from my sin.

3 For I know my transgressions, and my sin is ever before me.

4 Against You, You only, I have sinned and done what is evil in Your sight, So that You are justified when You speak And blameless when You judge.

5 Behold, I was brought forth in iniquity, and in sin my mother conceived me.

6 Behold, You desire truth in the innermost being, and in the hidden part You will make me know wisdom.

7 Purify me with hyssop, and I shall be clean; Wash me, and I shall be whiter than snow.

8 Make me to hear joy and gladness, Let the bones which You have broken rejoice.

9 Hide Your face from my sins And blot out all my iniquities.

10 Create in me a clean heart, O God, and renew a steadfast spirit within me.

11 Do not cast me away from Your presence and do not take Your Holy Spirit from me.

12 Restore to me the joy of Your salvation And sustain me with a willing spirit.

Leviticus 14:1-7

1 Then the LORD spoke to Moses, saying,

2 This shall be the law of the leper in the day of his cleansing. Now he shall be brought to the priest,

3 and the priest shall go out to the outside of the camp. Thus the priest shall look, and if the infection of leprosy has been healed in the leper,

4 then the priest shall give orders to take two live clean birds and cedar wood and a scarlet string and hyssop for the one who is to be cleansed.

5 "The priest shall also give orders to slay the one bird in an earthenware vessel over running water.

6 *As for* the live bird, he shall take it together with the cedar wood and the scarlet string and the hyssop, and shall dip them and the live bird in the blood of the bird that was slain over the running water.

7 "He shall then sprinkle seven times the one who is to be cleansed from the leprosy and shall pronounce him clean, and shall let the live bird go free over the open field."

Hebrews 13:11-13

11 For the bodies of those animals whose blood is brought into the holy place by the high priest *as an offering* for sin, are burned outside the camp.

12 Therefore Jesus also, that He might sanctify the people through His own blood, suffered outside the gate.

13 So, let us go out to Him outside the camp, bearing His reproach.

Isaiah 1:16-18

16 "Wash yourselves, make yourselves clean; Remove the evil of your deeds from My sight. Cease to do evil,

17 Learn to do good; seek justice, reprove the ruthless, defend the orphan, plead for the widow.

18 "Come now, and let us reason together," Says the LORD, "Though your sins are as scarlet, they will be as white as snow; though they are red like crimson, they will be like wool."

John 13:8-10

8 Peter said to Him, "Never shall You wash my feet!" Jesus answered him, "If I do not wash you, you have no part with Me."

9 Simon Peter said to Him, "Lord, *then wash* not only my feet, but also my hands and my head."

10 Jesus said to him, "He who has bathed needs only to wash his feet, but is completely clean; and you are clean, but not all of you."

John 10:10

10 "The thief comes only to steal and kill and destroy; I came that they may have life, and have it abundantly."

John 6:37

37 "All that the Father gives Me will come to Me, and the one who comes to Me I will certainly not cast out."

Hebrews 9:12, 10:10, 10:14

12 and not through the blood of goats and calves, but through His own blood, He entered the holy place once for all, having obtained eternal redemption.

10 By this will we have been sanctified through the offering of the body of Jesus Christ once for all.

14 For by one offering He has perfected for all time those who are sanctified.

What Does God Require For Forgiveness?

PROGRAM 36

TODAY'S TEXTS
Psalm 51:1-18
Jeremiah 13:11
Ephesians 1:13-14
Hebrews 13:5-6
Romans 5:1-8

INTRODUCTION

Is adultery a death knell to a marriage? It may be, but it doesn't have to be. Adultery leaves residuals. It leaves broken relationships. It leaves people hurt and wounded and wondering whether they can trust and there can be trust again. There can be restoration again. There can be renewal again. There can be a deliverance from those thoughts that torment you over your sin.

QUESTIONS

1. Review Psalm 51:1-18.

   a. What was the occasion for David writing this Psalm?

   b. Is there any hint in this passage that adulterers and murderers can't be forgiven and the restored?

   c. List what David asks God <u>not</u> to do *to* him.

   d. List what David asks God to do for him.

   e. Did David permanently lose his ministry? Write out the verses and phrases that show hope for his ministry to be restored in spite of the terrible things he did.

   f. Does God want our sacrifice or our heart? What kind of heart does He not despise?

2. From the following verses, what do we know about the Lord and about what He has done to secure our relationship with Him?

   a. Ephesians 1:13-14

   b. Hebrews 13:5-6

   c. Romans 5:1-8

3. If you or your spouse have committed adultery, how do these truths give you hope for restoration with the Lord and with your spouse?

Prayer

Father, thank You for teaching me how and what to pray. I'm so encouraged by David's prayer to see that the worst of sins against men, adultery and even murder, cannot permanently destroy relationships with You and with others. I ask You to blot out all my past iniquities, cleanse me thoroughly from these sins, create a new heart and a persevering spirit within me. Restore the joy of my salvation and cause my tongue to joyfully sing of Your righteousness given to us in Christ so I can teach unbelievers Your ways and they turn to You. In Jesus' name, Amen!

Today's Texts

Psalm 51:1-18

1 For the choir director. A Psalm of David, when Nathan the prophet came to him, after he had gone in to Bathsheba. Be gracious to me, O God, according to Your loving-kindness; according to the greatness of Your compassion blot out my transgressions.

2 Wash me thoroughly from my iniquity and cleanse me from my sin.

3 For I know my transgressions, and my sin is ever before me.

4 Against You, You only, I have sinned and done what is evil in Your sight, So that You are justified when You speak And blameless when You judge.

5 Behold, I was brought forth in iniquity, and in sin my mother conceived me.

6 Behold, You desire truth in the innermost being, and in the hidden part You will make me know wisdom.

7 Purify me with hyssop, and I shall be clean; Wash me, and I shall be whiter than snow.

8 Make me to hear joy and gladness, Let the bones which You have broken rejoice.

9 Hide Your face from my sins And blot out all my iniquities.

10 Create in me a clean heart, O God, and renew a steadfast spirit within me.

11 Do not cast me away from Your presence and do not take Your Holy Spirit from me.

12 Restore to me the joy of Your salvation And sustain me with a willing spirit.

13 Then I will teach transgressors Your ways, and sinners will be converted to You.

14 Deliver me from bloodguiltiness, O God, the God of my salvation; then my tongue will joyfully sing of Your righteousness.

15 O Lord, open my lips, that my mouth may declare Your praise.

16 For You do not delight in sacrifice, otherwise I would give it; You are not pleased with burnt offering.

17 The sacrifices of God are a broken spirit; a broken and a contrite heart, O God, You will not despise.

18 By Your favor do good to Zion; Build the walls of Jerusalem.

Jeremiah 13:11

11 'For as the waistband clings to the waist of a man, so I made the whole household of Israel and the whole household of Judah cling to Me,' declares the LORD, 'that they might be for Me a people, for renown, for praise and for glory; but they did not listen.'

Ephesians 1:13-14

13 In Him, you also, after listening to the message of truth, the gospel of your salvation-- having also believed, you were sealed in Him with the Holy Spirit of promise,

14 who is given as a pledge of our inheritance, with a view to the redemption of *God's own* possession, to the praise of His glory.

Hebrews 13:5-6

5 *Make sure that* your character is free from the love of money, being content with what you have; for He Himself has said, "I WILL NEVER DESERT YOU, NOR WILL I EVER FORSAKE YOU,"

6 so that we confidently say, "THE LORD IS MY HELPER, I WILL NOT BE AFRAID. WHAT WILL MAN DO TO ME?"

Romans 5:1-8

1 Therefore, having been justified by faith, we have peace with God through our Lord Jesus Christ,

2 through whom also we have obtained our introduction by faith into this grace in which we stand; and we exult in hope of the glory of God.

3 And not only this, but we also exult in our tribulations, knowing that tribulation brings about perseverance;

4 and perseverance, proven character; and proven character, hope;

5 and hope does not disappoint, because the love of God has been poured out within our hearts through the Holy Spirit who was given to us.

6 For while we were still helpless, at the right time Christ died for the ungodly.

7 For one will hardly die for a righteous man; though perhaps for the good man someone would dare even to die.

8 But God demonstrates His own love toward us, in that while we were yet sinners, Christ died for us.

PROGRAM **37**

TODAY'S TEXTS
Psalm 51:1-18

When You Have Sinned Against God

INTRODUCTION

You've committed adultery. You've come to your senses and you've said, "Oh my God, what have I done and what am I going to do?" How do you handle it with God? How do you handle it with your mate? How do you handle it with your children? Where do you begin? What are you going to do now that you've committed adultery? Well I want you to know that the Bible has a lot to say about adultery. And there is a way to handle it. There is a way of healing but you've got to take God's way.

QUESTIONS

1. Review Psalm 51:1-18. Find the verses that contradict the statements that follow. Then write in the verse number and key terms or phrases underneath.

   a. _____ God only *partially* washes off iniquity.

   b. _____ God wants us to be believers "on the outside" only.

   c. _____ The best we can hope for is a gray mix of good and bad attitudes and actions.

   d. _____ The Lord doesn't gift us with perseverance; that's something we have to do ourselves.

   e. _____ Because men create laws, we "sin" against men and society.

   f. _____ God either can't or doesn't want to "deliver" from murder.

g. _____ We can bury sins deep enough in our subconscious so they won't bother us.

h. _____ God loves tough, arrogant spirits.

i. _____ Salvation is dull (more than one here).

j. _____ God doesn't break bones. He restores only things we break.

k. _____ We can lose God's anointing and ministries permanently.

l. _____ Man is born neutral or good and so we're all good by nature.

m._____ I don't need God's power to praise (worship) Him.

n. _____ God prefers external works and rituals to a heart-to-heart relationship

Prayer

Father, what a great exercise to take the world's popular contradictions and contrast them with the truth of Your Word to see just how majestic it is and how loving You are! This Psalm of David has been such a great blessing to me. I plan to meditate on it daily and even memorize it. Thank You for so many precious and comforting truths and promises to free me from the guilt of my past and enable me to hope again. I know there are others who are hopelessly depressed either because they don't know You or they believe their sin can root You out of their lives forever. As I have been comforted by David's prayer, I want to tell them that their sin, no matter how great and prolonged, is not sovereign over You. You are always free to be gracious and compassionate; You forgive; You create a new heart and willing spirit. And You restore . . . relationships and ministries . . . what a wonderful truth that is to hear! Lord, send me out with this prayer to tell others how forgiving and powerful You are to mend broken hearts and restore relationships. In Jesus' name, Amen!

Today's Texts

Psalm 51:1-18

1 For the choir director. A Psalm of David, when Nathan the prophet came to him, after he had gone in to Bathsheba. Be gracious to me, O God, according to Your loving-kindness; according to the greatness of Your compassion blot out my transgressions.

2 Wash me thoroughly from my iniquity and cleanse me from my sin.

3 For I know my transgressions, and my sin is ever before me.

4 Against You, You only, I have sinned and done what is evil in Your sight, So that You are justified when You speak And blameless when You judge.

5 Behold, I was brought forth in iniquity, and in sin my mother conceived me.

6 Behold, You desire truth in the innermost being, and in the hidden part You will make me know wisdom.

7 Purify me with hyssop, and I shall be clean; Wash me, and I shall be whiter than snow.

8 Make me to hear joy and gladness, Let the bones which You have broken rejoice.

9 Hide Your face from my sins And blot out all my iniquities.

10 Create in me a clean heart, O God, and renew a steadfast spirit within me.

11 Do not cast me away from Your presence and do not take Your Holy Spirit from me.

12 Restore to me the joy of Your salvation And sustain me with a willing spirit.

13 Then I will teach transgressors Your ways, and sinners will be converted to You.

14 Deliver me from bloodguiltiness, O God, the God of my salvation; then my tongue will joyfully sing of Your righteousness.

15 O Lord, open my lips, that my mouth may declare Your praise.

16 For You do not delight in sacrifice, otherwise I would give it; You are not pleased with burnt offering.

17 The sacrifices of God are a broken spirit; a broken and a contrite heart, O God, You will not despise.

18 By Your favor do good to Zion; Build the walls of Jerusalem.

Untangling the Mess When Your Mate Has Committed Adultery

PROGRAM 38

TODAY'S TEXTS
Ezekiel 16:5-8, 32
Jeremiah 2:2, 20-25
Jeremiah 3:2
Deuteronomy 24:1-4
Matthew 19:9
1 Corinthians 7:15

INTRODUCTION

Your mate has committed adultery. You are angry. You are furious. "How could you do this?" Why did you do this?" You feel violated. Your trust has been broken. It seems like everything has been just shattered into smithereens. And you wonder, can we put it back together again? Is there anything we can do? Is there any hope? "How could you do this to our children?" And you're just frustrated.

QUESTIONS

1. Review the following verses. After each, briefly summarize God's "been-there, done-that" experience with His own adulterous wife, Israel.

   a. Ezekiel 16:5-8, 32

   b. Jeremiah 2:2, 20-25

2. Read Deuteronomy 24:1-4.

   a. If a man divorces his wife and she remarries, if her second husband rejects her, can her first husband take her back?

   b. Why or why not?

3. After each verse, write a key term that describes the exception that permits divorce.
   a. Matthew 19:9 _____

   b. 1 Corinthians 7:15 _____

4. Sometime read the entire 14-chapter book of Hosea marking every reference to **adultery** and **adulteress** with a red "A" and every reference to **harlotry** with a red "H."

   a. In what ways was Israel an adulteress and harlot?

   b. Referring to His faithless nation that went "a-whoring" (Exodus 34:15, 16; Judges 2:17; Hosea 4:12) after heathen gods, God says He "sent her away with a decree of divorce" (Jeremiah 3:8).

   1) According to Hosea, is His divorce permanent or does He plan to bring Old Faithless back?

   2) If He plans to bring her back, how will He do it? (See Hosea 2.)

   c. Is there a lesson in Hosea for us? Should we keep the door open to spouses who have abandoned us for others?

Prayer

Father, two things amaze me—Your faithfulness and Your people's faithlessness to Your Covenant. So much of Israel's history has been rebellion against Your truths and statutes; You showered them with so many blessings from heaven yet they defied Your holy laws and went "a-whorin" after the gods of heathen nations. Lord, remind me of these things if I'm ever so abandoned by the one I chose to wed. Help me take the beatings and not be vindictive. Keep me from becoming bitter beyond measure. Strengthen my patience and faith in Your sovereignty that more often resolves and restores things in the long-term. Remind me to be gracious and full of compassion as You always have been toward Your people in spite of their rebellion. Guard my heart from the strong "pull" of other gods and men so I don't entrap myself in adultery and fornication. In Jesus' name I pray, Amen!

Today's Texts

Ezekiel 16:5-8, 32

5 "No eye looked with pity on you to do any of these things for you, to have compassion on you. Rather you were thrown out into the open field, for you were abhorred on the day you were born.

6 "When I passed by you and saw you squirming in your blood, I said to you *while you were* in your blood, 'Live!' Yes, I said to you *while you were* in your blood, 'Live!'

7 "I made you numerous like plants of the field. Then you grew up, became tall and reached the age for fine ornaments; *your* breasts were formed and your hair had grown. Yet you were naked and bare.

8 "Then I passed by you and saw you, and behold, you were at the time for love; so I spread My skirt over you and covered your nakedness. I also swore to you and entered into a covenant with you so that you became Mine," declares the Lord GOD.

32 "You adulteress wife, who takes strangers instead of her husband!"

Jeremiah 2:2, 20-25

2 "Go and proclaim in the ears of Jerusalem, saying, 'Thus says the LORD, "I remember concerning you the devotion of your youth, The love of your betrothals, Your following after Me in the wilderness, Through a land not sown."

20 "For long ago I broke your yoke *and* tore off your bonds; but you said, 'I will not serve!' For on every high hill and under every green tree You have lain down as a harlot.

21 "Yet I planted you a choice vine, a completely faithful seed. How then have you turned yourself before Me into the degenerate shoots of a foreign vine?

22 "Although you wash yourself with lye and use much soap, the stain of your iniquity is before Me," declares the Lord GOD.

23 "How can you say, 'I am not defiled, I have not gone after the Baals'? Look at your way in the valley! Know what you have done! You are a swift young camel entangling her ways,

24 A wild donkey accustomed to the wilderness, that sniffs the wind in her passion. In *the time of* her heat who can turn her away? All who seek her will not become weary; in her month they will find her.

25 "Keep your feet from being unshod and your throat from thirst; But you said, 'It is hopeless! No! For I have loved strangers, and after them I will walk.'

Jeremiah 3:2

2 "Lift up your eyes to the bare heights and see; where have you not been violated? By the roads you have sat for them Like an Arab in the desert, and you have polluted a land with your harlotry and with your wickedness."

Deuteronomy 24:1-4

1 "When a man takes a wife and marries her, and it happens that she finds no favor in his eyes because he has found some indecency in her, and he writes her a certificate of divorce and puts it in her hand and sends her out from his house,

2 And she leaves his house and goes and becomes another man's wife,

3 and if the latter husband turns against her and writes her a certificate of divorce and puts it in her hand and sends her out of his house, or if the latter husband dies who took her to be his wife,

4 then her former husband who sent her away is not allowed to take her again to be his wife, since she has been defiled; for that is an abomination before the LORD, and you shall not bring sin on the land which the LORD your God gives you as an inheritance.

Matthew 19:9

9 "And I say to you, whoever divorces his wife, except for immorality, and marries another woman commits adultery."

1 Corinthians 7:15

15 Yet if the unbelieving one leaves, let him leave; the brother or the sister is not under bondage in such cases, but God has called us to peace.

My Mate Has Committed Adultery. How Can I Forgive?

PROGRAM 39

TODAY'S TEXTS
Jeremiah 3:12-13
Ephesians 4:26
Ezekiel 16:25, 59-62
Ephesians 4:31-32
Luke 23:34
Matthew 6:12, 14
Matthew 18:21-35

INTRODUCTION

Your mate has committed adultery!! And in the midst of that discovery, there's a pleading. "Please forgive me. I don't know what got into me. I don't know why I did it. I don't know what possessed me. All I know is I don't want you to leave and I don't want a divorce. I am so sorry for what I have done." Where do you go then?

QUESTIONS

1. Read Jeremiah 3:12-13.

   a. What does God command his "faithless" people?

   b. What does He promise and on what basis (attribute)?

   c. What does He "only" demand of them?

   d. How can we apply this "only" to reconciliation after divorce?

   e. Is it possible to be angry but not sin? (See Ephesians 4:26.)

2. Now read Ezekiel 16:25, 59-62.

   a. Who did Israel, God's wife, attempt to seduce?

   b. What does God threaten to do?

   c. Is this threat and punishment permanent? What does He further promise to do farther down the road?

   d. How will His wife respond to this love of His?

   e. Then what will He do?

3. What do the following scriptures teach us about forgiveness and anger?
   a. Ephesians 4:31-32.

   b. Luke 23:34

   c. Matthew 6:12-14

4. Now read the entire parable in Matthew 18:21-35.
   a. What did Peter ask?

   b. How did Jesus respond?

   c. How much did the first servant owe his master?

   d. What did his master threaten?

   e. How did he respond to this threat?

   f. What did his master do next?

   g. What did he do subsequently to his own servant?

   h. How do the two debts compare?

   i. What happened when his master caught him not having mercy?

   j. What was his punishment?

   k. How does Jesus conclude the parable in v. 35? Just how important is forgiveness? By analogy, how much do we "owe" God compared to what others "owe" us?

Prayer

Father, forgiveness is so hard when we have a legal claim and legitimate anger against people who have betrayed trust and broken covenant with us. I'm awed by Jesus' words "Forgive them, they know not what they do" from the very cross to His surrounding enemies. Lord, I know You love me in spite of my own idolatrous adultery—the "whoring" of my flesh after the gods of this world. I rest in Your promise to heal the apostasy of Your wife (Hosea 14:4) through the sanctification of Your Spirit so that we may be blameless in body, soul, and spirit on the Day of the Lord Jesus. Until then, help me unreservedly forgive the tally of minor offenses against me that so clearly contrast with my major offenses against You. Remind me daily of how much comparatively You have forgiven me for. In Jesus' name I pray, Amen!

Today's Texts

Jeremiah 3:12-13

12 "Go and proclaim these words toward the north and say, 'Return, faithless Israel,' declares the LORD; 'I will not look upon you in anger. For I am gracious,' declares the LORD; 'I will not be angry forever.

13 'Only acknowledge your iniquity, that you have transgressed against the LORD your God And have scattered your favors to the strangers under every green tree, and you have not obeyed My voice,' declares the LORD.

Ephesians 4:26

26 BE ANGRY, AND *yet* DO NOT SIN; do not let the sun go down on your anger,

Ezekiel 16:25, 59-62

25 "You built yourself a high place at the top of every street and made your beauty abominable, and you spread your legs to every passer-by to multiply your harlotry."

59 For thus says the Lord GOD, "I will also do with you as you have done, you who have despised the oath by breaking the covenant.

60 "Nevertheless, I will remember My covenant with you in the days of your youth, and I will establish an everlasting covenant with you.

61 "Then you will remember your ways and be ashamed when you receive your sisters, both your older and your younger; and I will give them to you as daughters, but not because of your covenant.

62 "Thus I will establish My covenant with you, and you shall know that I am the LORD,"

Ephesians 4:31-32

31 Let all bitterness and wrath and anger and clamor and slander be put away from you, along with all malice.

32 Be kind to one another, tender-hearted, forgiving each other, just as God in Christ also has forgiven you.

Luke 23:34

34 But Jesus was saying, "Father, forgive them; for they do not know what they are doing." And they cast lots, dividing up His garments among themselves.

Matthew 6:12, 14

12 'And forgive us our debts, as we also have forgiven our debtors.

14 'For if you forgive others for their transgressions, your heavenly Father will also forgive you.'

Matthew 18:21-35

21 Then Peter came and said to Him, "Lord, how often shall my brother sin against me and I forgive him? Up to seven times?"

22 Jesus said to him, "I do not say to you, up to seven times, but up to seventy times seven.

23 "For this reason the kingdom of heaven may be compared to a king who wished to settle accounts with his slaves.

24 "When he had begun to settle them, one who owed him ten thousand talents was brought to him.

25 "But since he did not have the means to repay, his lord commanded him to be sold, along with his wife and children and all that he had, and repayment to be made.

26 "So the slave fell to the ground and prostrated himself before him, saying, 'Have patience with me and I will repay you everything.'

27 "And the lord of that slave felt compassion and released him and forgave him the debt.

28 "But that slave went out and found one of his fellow slaves who owed him a hundred denarii; and he seized him and began to choke him, saying, 'Pay back what you owe.'

29 "So his fellow slave fell to the ground and began to plead with him, saying, 'Have patience with me and I will repay you.'

30 "But he was unwilling and went and threw him in prison until he should pay back what was owed.

31 "So when his fellow slaves saw what had happened, they were deeply grieved and came and reported to their lord all that had happened.

32 "Then summoning him, his lord said to him, 'You wicked slave, I forgave you all that debt because you pleaded with me.

33 'Should you not also have had mercy on your fellow slave, in the same way that I had mercy on you?'

34 "And his lord, moved with anger, handed him over to the torturers until he should repay all that was owed him."

35 "My heavenly Father will also do the same to you, if each of you does not forgive his brother from your heart."

Practical Steps For Reconciliation

PROGRAM 40

TODAY'S TEXTS
2 Corinthians 2:6-7
1 Corinthians 13:5
Proverbs 17:9
Ephesians 5:12
Proverbs 19:11
Ecclesiastes 9:9
2 Corinthians 10:4
Philippians 4:8

INTRODUCTION

He's the God of resurrection. He's the God of new beginnings. He's the God of hope. He's the God of healing. He's the God of encouragement. Just keep yourself in the Word of God and he will heal you both. And in the long run you can be stronger than you ever were before if you will just listen to God.

QUESTIONS

1. Read 2 Corinthians 2:6-7.

    a. Is it possible to over-punish someone for a past sin?

    b. What is the threat of over-punishment? What should we try to avoid?

    c. What should we do instead?

2. According to 1 Corinthians 13:5, what four characteristics of love are peculiarly aimed at reconciliation? Are these easy to "pull off"?

    a. _____

    b. _____

    c. _____

    d. _____

3. Read Proverbs 17:9. Write down the actions that correspond to the motives noted:

    a. Seeks love by _____

    b. Separates intimate friends by _____

    c. Explain how each action can either advance or work against long-term reconciliation.

    d. According to Ephesians 5:12 are there "matters" that should not be publically disclosed? Is it wise to keep things under wraps? Why?

4. Read Proverbs 19:11.

   a. What does a man need to restrain his anger?

   b. What is one "glory" he should pursue? How?

5. What does Solomon recommend in Ecclesiastes 9:9?

6. According to 2 Corinthians 10:4 are we "on our own" in dealing with life's harshest situations? How does the Word of God help us deal with the worst?

7. What should we put our minds on according to Philippians 4:8?

Prayer

Father, thank You for these concluding practical steps for reconciliation from Your Word. I know from Your Word that our natural actions are done primarily from a spirit of competition (Ecclesiastes 4:4) and so it's natural for us to expose, rather than conceal, the transgressions and failures of others and withhold praise. Rather than forgive and comfort, we tend to overwhelm the guilty with excessive sorrow, reminding people of bad things they've done. Lord, help me put to death this natural motive and behavior of my flesh. Cause me to forgive and comfort, to overlook and conceal sins, to consider others higher than myself, and to praise what is praiseworthy in others because You've made it happen. Help me put my mind on truth, honor, justice, purity, loveliness, good reputation, excellence and things worthy of praise . . . generally . . . on things above. In Jesus' name, Amen!

Today's Texts

2 Corinthians 2:6-7

6 Sufficient for such a one is this punishment which was inflicted by the majority,

7 so that on the contrary you should rather forgive and comfort him, otherwise such a one might be overwhelmed by excessive sorrow.

1 Corinthians 13:5

5 does not act unbecomingly; it does not seek its own, is not provoked, does not take into account a wrong suffered,

Proverbs 17:9

9 He who conceals a transgression seeks love, but he who repeats a matter separates intimate friends.

Ephesians 5:12

12 for it is disgraceful even to speak of the things which are done by them in secret.

Proverbs 19:11

11 A man's discretion makes him slow to anger, and it is his glory to overlook a transgression.

Ecclesiastes 9:9

9 Enjoy life with the woman whom you love all the days of your fleeting life which He has given to you under the sun; for this is your reward in life and in your toil in which you have labored under the sun.

2 Corinthians 10:4

4 for the weapons of our warfare are not of the flesh, but divinely powerful for the destruction of fortresses.

Philippians 4:8

8 Finally, brethren, whatever is true, whatever is honorable, whatever is right, whatever is pure, whatever is lovely, whatever is of good repute, if there is any excellence and if anything worthy of praise, dwell on these things.

DISCOVER TRUTH FOR YOURSELF

Our passion is for you to discover Truth for yourself through Inductive Bible Study—a unique Bible study method you'll discover in the following pages and use throughout this study, as we engage this important topic together verse by verse.

You can't do a better thing than sit at Jesus' feet, listening to His every word. God's Word, the Bible, has answers for every situation you'll face in life. Listen to what God is saying to you, face-to-face, with truth to transform your life!

INDUCTIVE BIBLE STUDY METHOD

To study and understand God's Word, we use the Inductive Bible Study Method at Precept Ministries International. The Bible is our main source of truth. Before looking for insights from people and commentaries *about* the Bible, we get into the Word of God, beginning with observing the text.

❶ Observation

This is a very interactive process, well worth the time because the truths you discover for yourself will be accurate and profound. It begins by asking the five W and H questions.

Who is speaking? Who is this about? Who are the main characters? And to whom is the speaker speaking?

What subjects and/or events are covered in the chapter? What do you learn about the people, the events, and the teachings from the text? What instructions are given?

When did or will the events recorded occur?

Where did or will this happen? Where was it said?

Why is something said? Why will an event occur? Why this time, person, and/or place?

How will it happen? How will it be done? How is it illustrated?

Careful observation leads to interpretation—discovering what the text means.

❷ Interpretation

The more you observe, the greater you'll understand God's Word. Since Scripture is the best interpreter of Scripture, you and I will be looking at contexts and cross-references to enhance our understanding of the meaning of God's message.

Where should observation and interpretation lead? Application.

❸ Application

After we've observed the text and discovered what it means, we need to think and live accordingly. The result is a transformed life—the more you and I are in the Word of God and adjusting our thinking and behavior to its precepts for life, the more we are changed into the likeness of Jesus Christ! He is the living Word of God who became flesh, the Savior of the world, our coming King of kings!

SO WHERE DO YOU BEGIN?

The Bible is *God's* book, His Word, so when you study it you need to seek the Author's help. Begin with prayer, asking God to lead you into all truth, then open the Study Companion. (We suggest you work one program ahead of the broadcast to get the most out of the study.) Look at the general layout of each day's program and you will find the following:

- Introduction—usually with a challenging question
- Questions that contain pointers on using the Inductive Bible Study Method
- **Where's That Verse?** section containing the Primary Study Passage and several cross-references related to the topic
- Concluding Prayer

WHAT'S NEXT?

- In some programs, I'll point out key words to mark. You'll find many of them on the back cover of this Study Companion with *suggested* colors and symbols to spot them quickly in the text. Color coding key words helps you identify and recall. We have included a cutout bookmark so you can remember to mark each key word the same way throughout the text.

  You can mark these key words before or after the program, whichever is easier. You can also get the CD or DVD of the program and mark the key words later while studying.

Feel free to mark them your own way—there's nothing sacred about the particular symbols and colors I use!

- The cross-references I mention in these programs are under **Where's That Verse?** After you read them, you can jot them in the margins of the **Observation Worksheets** or write them in the wide margins of your Bible. I suggest you first pencil them in, then write them in ink later.

- For book studies, you'll find an **At A Glance** chart in the back. After we complete a chapter, record a summary theme there and in the space provided in your **Observation Worksheets**. Themes help you remember main ideas of chapters **At A Glance** after you finish the study. You'll also find these charts after each book in the *New Inductive Study Bible*.

MISSED A PROGRAM?

- Go to our website at **www.PreceptsForLife.com**. TV viewers can call 1.800.763.1990 and radio listeners 1.888.734.7707 to learn how to find programs online.

GETTING THE MOST FROM THIS STUDY

- Try to stay one program ahead of me so you'll learn directly from the Word of God and our time together will be like a "discussion group," as we reason together through the Scriptures. You'll get much more out of our time together if you've done this preparation.

- Try to memorize a key verse for every program covered. God will bring these to your remembrance when you need them!

- Pray about what you learn each day. Ask God to remind you of these truths and give you another person to share them with. These two exercises will do amazing things in your life.

- Get the CD or DVD set of this series and listen when you get ready for work in the morning, do chores around the house, or have family devotions. Or listen with an open Bible and discuss the teaching and its application to your life. Get together with a friend, view or listen to a message, and discuss it or use it for family devotions. You can also view or listen programs online. Visit **www.PreceptsForLife.com.**

- Request Precept's mailings to stay abreast of what God is doing around the world and to pray for the needs we share with you. You can be a significant part of this unique global ministry God is using to establish people in His Word. Here are some items you can request:

  ✦ The *Plumbline*—Precept Ministry's monthly e-newsletter that keeps you up to date on Bible study topics, products and events that help you in your walk with Christ.

  ✦ A prayer list so you can partner with us in prayer for our ministries in nearly 150 countries and 70 languages.

  ✦ "Inside information" each month when you join our "E-Team" of regular prayer and financial supporters. Visit **www.PreceptsForLife.com** for more information on how you can support our programs. (You can check out the current monthly letter right now on our website.)

  ✦ Advance notice of conferences at our headquarters in Chattanooga and throughout the United States and Canada.

  ✦ Information about our study tours in Israel, Jordan, Greece, Turkey, and Italy, where we teach various books of the Bible right where the action occurred!

- We use one of the most accurate translations of the Bible, the New American Standard (Updated). If the topic is a book study, our **Observation Worksheets** will contain the complete text. Since you'll be instructed to mark words and phrases and make notes in the text, you'll want to have colored pencils or pens available. As you grow in inductive study skills, you may want to use your Bible instead. We believe the best Bible to use is the *New Inductive Study Bible*. See our back pages to find out more about this ultimate study Bible. Now get started!

- Finally, stay in touch with me personally. I'd so love to hear from you by email or letter so I can be sensitive to where you are and what you're experiencing—problems you're wrestling with, questions you have, etc. This will help me teach more effectively and personally. Just email us at info@precept.org. (Don't worry, Beloved, I won't mention you by name; but as you listen, you'll know I've heard you!)

I'm committed to you . . . because of Him. The purpose of the "Precepts For Life" TV & Radio programs is to help you realize your full potential in God, so you can become the exemplary believer God intends you to be...studying the Bible inductively, viewing the world biblically, making disciples intentionally, and serving the Church faithfully in the power of the Holy Spirit."

That's my vision for us as believers! Won't you help us spread it to others?

Looking for people...looking for truth!

How Do I Start Studying The Bible?

Do you wonder,
God, how can I obey You and study your Word? Where do I begin? How can I discover truth for myself?

DISCOVER TRUTH FOR YOURSELF

There are some study tools we would recommend for you to begin with, as each will teach you the inductive method of study. By inductive we mean that you can go straight to the Word of God and discover truth for yourself, so you can say … "for You, Yourself have taught me" (Psalm 119:102).

Let's Get Started! For a jump start on inductive study, we recommend the following:

- *Lord, Teach Me To Study The Bible in 28 Days.* In this hands-on introduction to the basics of inductive study, you'll see why you need to study God's Word and how to dig into the truths of a book of the Bible. The instructions will walk you through the books of Jonah and Jude, and you'll be awed at what you see on your own! Discussion questions are included.

- *God, Are You There? Do You Care? Do You Know About Me?* This 13-week, self-contained inductive study on the Gospel of John is powerful and life-changing. Study the book of John, as you learn and put into practice inductive study skills. The Gospel of John was written that you might believe that Jesus is the Son of God and that believing, might have life in His name. You will know you are loved! Discussion questions are included.

- *How to Study Old Testament History and Prophecy Workshop.* Discover truths about who God is and how He works as you learn to study inductively, step by step, and be challenged to apply these truths to your life. This workshop will give you the tools to study and understand Old Testament history and prophecy. Go to www.precept.org or call 800-763-8280 to find out about workshops in your area, or online training.

- *How to Study a New Testament Letter Workshop.* Grow in the knowledge of the Lord Jesus Christ and His plan for your life. This inductive study workshop will equip you to study the New Testament letters and apply their truths to your life. Go to www.precept.org or call 800-763-8280 to find out about workshops in your area, or online training.

Now that you've begun . . . continue studying inductively using one of these:

- *40 Minute Bible Studies.* These 6-week topical studies are a good for personal study and a great way to start discipling others one-on-one or in a group setting—teaching them who God is, introducing them to Jesus Christ, and helping them learn God's precepts for life. These studies enable you to discover what God says about different issues of life. No homework is necessary for the students prior to group time.

- *The New Inductive Study Series,* now complete covering every book of the Bible, was created to help you discover truth for yourself and go deeper into God's precepts, promises and purposes. This powerful series is ideal for personal study, small groups,

Sunday school classes, family devotions, and discipling others. Containing 13-week long studies, the New Inductive Study Series also provides easy planning for church curriculum! You can now survey the entire Bible

- ***Lord Series.*** These life-changing devotional studies cover in greater depth major issues of our relationship with God and with others, teaching us how to practically live out our faith. Ideal for small groups, these contain discussion guides and teaching DVDs are available for some.

- ***Discover 4 Yourself*** is a dynamic series of inductive studies for children. Children who can read learn how to discover truth for themselves through the life-impacting skills of observation, interpretation, and application. You'll be amazed at the change that comes when children know for themselves what the Word of God says! Teach them now so they can stand firm in a first-hand knowledge of truth as they hit their teen years. This award-winning series is popular in Christian schools and among homeschoolers. Teacher's guides are available online.

- ***The New Inductive Study Bible (NISB)*** is a unique and exciting! Most study Bibles give you someone else's interpretation of the text. The NISB doesn't tell you what to believe, rather it helps you discover truth for yourself by showing you how to study inductively and providing instructions, study helps, and application questions for each book of the Bible, as well as wide margins for your notes. It's filled with many wonderful features that will guide you toward the joy of discovering the truths of God's Word for yourself. This Bible is your legacy.

GO DEEPER WITH OTHERS… IN SMALL GROUP BIBLE STUDIES

Join others in the study of God's Word, sharing insights from the Scripture and discussing application to your life. Each of the studies described above are appropriate for groups as well as for individual study.

Discussion questions are included, so that you can dialogue about what you're learning with a group. These studies will teach you what it means to live by God's Word—and how it is applied to life. Learn about and discuss with others the truth that sets you free! To find out about inductive Bible study groups in your area, go to www.precept.org or call 800-763-8280.

DISCIPLE

How can you help others study God's Word inductively? Use the studies described above to share with others—one-on-one or in a small group. Lead others in discovering truth for themselves and experience the joy of seeing God change lives!

If you want training in how to lead these and other Precept Upon Precept studies go to www.precept.org or call us at 800-763-8280.

**Precept Ministries International | P.O. Box 182218 | Chattanooga, TN 37422
800.763.8280 | www.precept.org**

About Precept

Precept Ministries International was raised up by God for the sole purpose of establishing people in God's Word to produce reverence for Him. It serves as an arm of the church without respect to denomination. God has enabled Precept to reach across denominational lines without compromising the truths of His inerrant Word. We believe every word of the Bible was inspired and given to man as all that is necessary for him to become mature and thoroughly equipped for every good work of life. This ministry does not seek to impose its doctrines on others, but rather to direct people to the Master Himself, who leads and guides by His Spirit into all truth through a systematic study of His Word. The ministry produces a variety of Bible studies and holds conferences and intensive Training Workshops designed to establish attendees in the Word through Inductive Bible Study.

Jack Arthur and his wife, Kay, founded Precept Ministries in 1970. Kay and the ministry staff of writers produce **Precept Upon Precept** studies, **In & Out** studies, **Lord** series studies, the **New Inductive Study Series** studies, **40-Minute** studies, and **Discover 4 Yourself Inductive Bible Studies for Kids**. From years of diligent study and teaching experience, Kay and the staff have developed these unique, inductive courses that are now used in nearly 180 countries and 70 languages

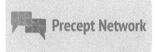 Precept Network is an interconnected, committed group of volunteers passionately using their gifts and abilities to accomplish the mission of establishing people in God's Word!

In support of this mission, Precept Network Area Teams launched in the summer of 2012! The goal of these teams is to connect and equip Bible Study Leaders in their local communities to impact others with the life-transforming study of God's Word through the Inductive Bible Study Method. The Area Teams will provide support in states across the country. Please be in prayer for the teams as they branch out in faith to reach more and more people. If you would like to see if there is an Area Team near you, visit www.precept.org/areateams for a list of the current teams and their locations. If you do not find an Area Team close to you, you can find Bible Study Leader Enrichment Groups in our Precept Online Community. For more information, go to www.precept.org/poc.

 Now that you've studied and prayerfully considered the scriptures, is there something new for you to believe or do, or did it move you to make a change in your life? It's one of the many amazing and supernatural results of being in His life-changing Word—God speaks to us.

At Precept Ministries International, we believe that we have heard God speak about our part in the Great Commission. He has told us in His Word to make disciples by teaching people how to study His Word. We plan to reach 10 million people with Inductive Bible Study.

If you share our passion for establishing people in God's Word, we invite you to join us! Will you prayerfully consider joining our E-Team and giving monthly to the ministry? If you give an online recurring gift as an E-Team member, fewer dollars go into administrative costs and more go toward ministry. You can join the E-Team at www.precept.org/eteam. You can also make a one-time gift to reach more people with Inductive Bible Study at www.precept.org/ATC. Please pray about how the Lord might lead you to answer the call.

 When you buy books, studies, videos and audios, please purchase from Precept Ministries through our online store (**http://store.precept.org/**). We realize you may find some of these materials at a lower price through for-profit retailers, but when you buy through us, the proceeds support the work that we do to:

- Develop new Inductive Bible studies
- Translate more studies into other languages
- Support efforts in nearly 185 countries
- Reach millions daily through radio and television
- Train pastors and Bible Study Leaders around the world

- Develop inductive studies for children to start their journey with God
- Equip people of all ages with Bible Study skills that transform lives

When you buy from Precept, you help to establish people in God's Word!

Concerned you might miss a program?

Don't be! You can get a CD or DVD of this program and mark the Observation Worksheets as you study at your own pace. It will be like going to God's Bible school and having the Holy Spirit as your professor. He will take the things of God and reveal them to you.

TV viewers, call 1.800.763.1990, radio listeners, call 1.888.734.7707! We'll be happy to place an order for you!

You can also listen to or watch the programs online whenever you want on our website **www.PreceptsForLife.com.**

40-Minutes a Week Could Change Your Life

Marriage begins with visions of eternal love, hope, and happiness. Yet, even among Christians, hope too quickly fades. The happiness dims. And love seems too hard to sustain.

It doesn't have to be that way. God designed marriage to be a satisfying, fulfilling relationship, and He created men and women so that they-together, and as one flesh-could reflect His love for the world. Marriage, when lived out as God intended, makes us complete, it brings us joy, and gives our lives fresh meaning.

These revolutionary, no-homework, 6-week studies are an easy introduction to inductive study. They have proven great for small groups and have a unique format that includes Scripture alongside the text. Zoom in on the issues you care about and learn to think about them as God does.

40-MINUTE BIBLE STUDIES

Building a Marriage That Really Works

www.preceptsforlife.com
ONLINE

1.800.763.1990
TELEVISION

1.888.734.7707
RADIO

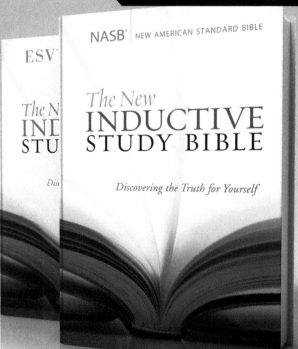

Printed in the USA
CPSIA information can be obtained
at www.ICGtesting.com
LVHW051640181023
761321LV00013B/281